LAWS AND LEGISLATION

THE UNITED NATIONS CONVENTION ON THE RIGHTS OF PERSONS WITH DISABILITIES AND U.S. RATIFICATION ISSUES

LAWS AND LEGISLATION

Additional books in this series can be found on Nova's website under the Series tab.

Additional E-books in this series can be found on Nova's website under the E-book tab.

DISABILITY AND THE DISABLED-ISSUES, LAWS AND PROGRAMS

Additional books in this series can be found on Nova's website under the Series tab.

Additional E-books in this series can be found on Nova's website under the E-book tab.

LAWS AND LEGISLATION

THE UNITED NATIONS CONVENTION ON THE RIGHTS OF PERSONS WITH DISABILITIES AND U.S. RATIFICATION ISSUES

TIMO WALLNER
EDITOR

nova publishers
New York

For permission to use material from this book please contact us:
Telephone 631-231-7269; Fax 631-231-8175
Web Site: http://www.novapublishers.com

Library of Congress Cataloging-in-Publication Data

ISBN: 978-1-62808-120-6

Published by Nova Science Publishers, Inc. † New York

CONTENTS

PREFACE

During the 113th Congress, the Senate might consider providing its advice and consent to ratification of the U.N. Convention on the Rights of Persons with Disabilities (CRPD). CRPD, which has been ratified or acceded to by 129 countries, is a multilateral agreement that addresses the rights of disabled persons. Its purpose is to promote, protect, and ensure the full and equal enjoyment of all human rights and fundamental freedoms by persons with disabilities. Many U.S. policymakers, including President Obama and some Members of Congress, agree that existing U.S. laws and policies are compatible with CRPD. In fact, some CRPD provisions appear to be modeled after U.S. disability laws. The United States has historically recognized the rights of individuals with disabilities through various laws and policies, including the Americans with Disabilities Act. This book provides an overview on the United Nations Convention on the Rights of Persons with Disabilities, with a focus on its objectives, structure, and policy issues.

Chapter 1 - During the 113th Congress, the Senate might consider providing its advice and consent to ratification of the U.N. Convention on the Rights of Persons with Disabilities (CRPD, or the Convention). CRPD, which has been ratified or acceded to by 129 countries, is a multilateral agreement that addresses the rights of disabled persons. Its purpose is to promote, protect, and ensure the full and equal enjoyment of all human rights and fundamental freedoms by persons with disabilities.

Many U.S. policymakers, including President Obama and some Members of Congress, agree that existing U.S. laws and policies are compatible with CRPD. In fact, some CRPD provisions appear to be modeled after U.S. disability laws. The United States has historically recognized the rights of individuals with disabilities through various laws and policies, including the Americans with Disabilities Act.

In July 2009, President Obama signed CRPD. The Administration transmitted it to the Senate for advice and consent to ratification in May 2012. The Senate Committee on Foreign Relations (SFRC) held a hearing on the Convention in July 2012 and later that month reported the treaty favorably to the full Senate by a vote of 13 in favor and 6 against, subject to certain conditions. In December 2012, the Senate voted against providing advice and consent to ratification of CRPD by a vote of 61 to 38. The treaty was automatically returned to SFRC at the end of the 112th Congress.

In debates regarding U.S. ratification of CRPD, the treaty's possible impact on U.S. sovereignty has been a key area of concern. Critics of the Convention maintain that treaties are the "supreme Law of the Land" under the Constitution, and that U.S. ratification of CRPD could supersede federal, state, and local laws. Supporters assert that CRPD is a non-discrimination treaty that does not create new obligations. They contend that U.S. laws meet, and in some cases exceed, CRPD requirements. Debate may also center on the following issues:

- **Role of the CPRD committee**. Critics are concerned that recommendations of the Committee on the Rights of Persons with Disabilities, the Convention's monitoring body, could deem U.S. laws to be in violation of CRPD and presume authority over the private lives of U.S. citizens. Supporters, including the Obama Administration, emphasize that committee decisions are non-binding under international and domestic law.
- **Possible impact on U.S. citizens and businesses abroad.** Some CRPD proponents contend that U.S. ratification may (1) improve the lives of U.S. citizens with disabilities living, working, or traveling abroad, and (2) "level the playing field" for U.S. companies that, unlike many of their foreign counterparts, already comply with higher disability standards. The extent to which U.S. ratification of CRPD may positively affect U.S. businesses or disabled U.S. citizens living or traveling abroad remains unclear.
- **Role in U.S. foreign policy.** Supporters contend that U.S. ratification may enhance U.S. credibility as it advocates the rights of persons with disabilities globally. Opponents argue that existing U.S. laws and policies are robust enough examples of U.S. commitment to the issue.

- **Abortion.** Some critics worry that the term “sexual and reproductive health” in CRPD could be a euphemism for abortion. Supporters note that the word “abortion” is never mentioned in CRPD and contend that no U.S laws related to abortion would be created as a result of U.S. ratification.
- **Parental rights.** Some are concerned that the U.S. ratification may give governments, and not U.S. parents, the right to make educational and treatment-related decisions for their disabled children. Others, including the Obama Administration, hold that existing federal, state, and local laws protect parental rights.

Other issues that Senators may wish to consider include challenges to evaluating CRPD’s effectiveness, obstacles to CRPD implementation, and the role and participation of civil society in CRPD mechanisms.

Chapter 2 – This is the Testimony of Judith Heumann, Special Adviser for International Disability Rights, U.S. Department of State. Hearing on "Convention on the Rights of Persons with Disabilities."

Chapter 3 – This is the Statement of Eve Hill, Senior Counselor to the Assistant Attorney General For Civil Rights, U.S. Department of Justice. Hearing on "Convention on the Rights of Persons with Disabilities."

Chapter 4 – This is the Testimony of Dick Thornburgh, Former Attorney General of the United States. Hearing on "Convention on the Rights of Persons with Disabilities."

Chapter 5 - This is the Testimony of John L. Wodatch, Former Chief of the Disability Rights Section, Civil Rights Division, U.S. Department of Justice. Hearing on "Convention on the Rights of Persons with Disabilities."

Chapter 6 – This is the Statement of Steven Groves, Bernard and Barbara Lomas Fellow, The Heritage Foundation. Hearing on "Convention on the Rights of Persons with Disabilities."

Chapter 7 – This is the Testimony of Michael Farris, Chancellor, Patrick Henry College. Hearing on "Convention on the Rights of Persons with Disabilities."

Chapter 8 – This is the Testimony of John Lancaster, Retired Executive Director, National Council On Independent Living. Hearing on "Convention on the Rights of Persons with Disabilities."

Chapter 9 – The Americans with Disabilities Act (ADA) provides broad nondiscrimination protection in employment, public services, public accommodations, services operated by public entities, transportation, and telecommunications for individuals with disabilities. This report summarizes the major provisions of the ADA and analyzes selected recent issues, including the Supreme Court cases and the ADA Amendments Act of 2008.

Chapter 10 - The consideration of treaties and nominations constitutes the executive business of the Senate. To conduct executive business, the Senate must resolve into executive session. Senate Rule XXIX governs executive sessions, generally; Rule XXX addresses proceedings on treaties.

When the President submits a treaty to the Senate, the treaty, and any supporting materials, are referred to the Committee on Foreign Relations. Paragraph 3 of Senate Rule XXIX requires that all treaties and "all remarks, votes, and proceedings thereon shall also be kept secret, until the Senate shall, by their resolution, take off the injunction of secrecy." At the time the treaty is referred to committee, the Senate typically agrees by unanimous consent to remove the "injunction of secrecy."

The Foreign Relations Committee can order the treaty reported back to the Senate—favorably, unfavorably, or without recommendation—or, instead, decline to act on the treaty. If the committee does not act on the treaty, it is not automatically returned to the President. Treaties, unlike bills and other legislative measures, remain available to the Senate from one Congress to the next, until they are disposed or the Senate agrees to return them to the President. Paragraph 2 of Rule XXX states in part that "all proceedings on treaties shall terminate with the Congress, and they shall be resumed at the commencement of the next Congress as if no proceedings had previously been had thereon." Thus, if the Foreign Relations Committee fails to report a treaty before the end of a Congress, the treaty remains before the committee during the next Congress. If the committee has reported a treaty, but the Senate has not completed floor consideration of it when the Congress ends, the treaty is recommitted to the committee, and the committee must report it again before the Senate may consider it on the floor.

In: The United Nations Convention …
Editor: Timo Wallner
ISBN: 978-1-62808-120-6

Chapter 1

THE UNITED NATIONS CONVENTION ON THE RIGHTS OF PERSONS WITH DISABILITIES: ISSUES IN THE U.S. RATIFICATION DEBATE*

Luisa Blanchfield, Cynthia Brougher and James V. DeBergh

SUMMARY

During the 113th Congress, the Senate might consider providing its advice and consent to ratification of the U.N. Convention on the Rights of Persons with Disabilities (CRPD, or the Convention). CRPD, which has been ratified or acceded to by 129 countries, is a multilateral agreement that addresses the rights of disabled persons. Its purpose is to promote, protect, and ensure the full and equal enjoyment of all human rights and fundamental freedoms by persons with disabilities.

Many U.S. policymakers, including President Obama and some Members of Congress, agree that existing U.S. laws and policies are compatible with CRPD. In fact, some CRPD provisions appear to be modeled after U.S. disability laws. The United States has historically recognized the rights of individuals with disabilities through various laws and policies, including the Americans with Disabilities Act.

---

* This is an edited, reformatted and augmented version of Congressional Research Service, Publication No. R42749, dated March 4, 2013.

In July 2009, President Obama signed CRPD. The Administration transmitted it to the Senate for advice and consent to ratification in May 2012. The Senate Committee on Foreign Relations (SFRC) held a hearing on the Convention in July 2012 and later that month reported the treaty favorably to the full Senate by a vote of 13 in favor and 6 against, subject to certain conditions. In December 2012, the Senate voted against providing advice and consent to ratification of CRPD by a vote of 61 to 38. The treaty was automatically returned to SFRC at the end of the 112th Congress.

In debates regarding U.S. ratification of CRPD, the treaty's possible impact on U.S. sovereignty has been a key area of concern. Critics of the Convention maintain that treaties are the "supreme Law of the Land" under the Constitution, and that U.S. ratification of CRPD could supersede federal, state, and local laws. Supporters assert that CRPD is a non-discrimination treaty that does not create new obligations. They contend that U.S. laws meet, and in some cases exceed, CRPD requirements. Debate may also center on the following issues:

- **Role of the CPRD committee**. Critics are concerned that recommendations of the Committee on the Rights of Persons with Disabilities, the Convention's monitoring body, could deem U.S. laws to be in violation of CRPD and presume authority over the private lives of U.S. citizens. Supporters, including the Obama Administration, emphasize that committee decisions are non-binding under international and domestic law.
- **Possible impact on U.S. citizens and businesses abroad.** Some CRPD proponents contend that U.S. ratification may (1) improve the lives of U.S. citizens with disabilities living, working, or traveling abroad, and (2) "level the playing field" for U.S. companies that, unlike many of their foreign counterparts, already comply with higher disability standards. The extent to which U.S. ratification of CRPD may positively affect U.S. businesses or disabled U.S. citizens living or traveling abroad remains unclear.
- **Role in U.S. foreign policy.** Supporters contend that U.S. ratification may enhance U.S. credibility as it advocates the rights of persons with disabilities globally. Opponents argue that existing U.S. laws and policies are robust enough examples of U.S. commitment to the issue.
- **Abortion.** Some critics worry that the term "sexual and reproductive health" in CRPD could be a euphemism for abortion. Supporters note that the word "abortion" is never mentioned in CRPD and contend that no U.S laws related to abortion would be created as a result of U.S. ratification.
- **Parental rights.** Some are concerned that the U.S. ratification may give governments, and not U.S. parents, the right to make

educational and treatment-related decisions for their disabled children. Others, including the Obama Administration, hold that existing federal, state, and local laws protect parental rights.

Other issues that Senators may wish to consider include challenges to evaluating CRPD's effectiveness, obstacles to CRPD implementation, and the role and participation of civil society in CRPD mechanisms.

INTRODUCTION

The Senate may consider providing its advice and consent to U.S. ratification of the United Nations (U.N.) Convention on the Rights of Persons with Disabilities (CRPD, or the Convention) during the 113th Congress. CRPD is the only multilateral treaty that specifically aims to protect the rights of those who are disabled. To date, 129 countries have ratified or acceded to the Convention. It has been signed by 155 countries, including the United States.

President Barack Obama signed CRPD on behalf of the United States on July 30, 2009. He transmitted it to the Senate for advice and consent to ratification in May 2012, where it was received and referred to the Committee on Foreign Relations (SFRC). The committee reported the Convention favorably to the full Senate on July 31, 2012, by a vote of 13 in favor and 6 against, subject to three reservations, eight understandings and two declarations.[2] On December 4, the full Senate voted against providing advice and consent to ratification of CRPD by a vote of 61 to 38. When the 112th Congress adjourned, the treaty was automatically returned to SFRC. The committee must report the treaty out again in order for the Senate to consider it.

U.S. Process for Making Multilateral Treaties

The making of multilateral treaties for the United States generally involves a series of steps in the following order: (1) negotiation and conclusion; (2) signing by the President; (3) transmittal to the Senate by the President, which may include any proposed reservations, declarations, and understandings; (4) referral to the Senate Committee on Foreign Relations; (5) committee consideration and report to the Senate recommending approval and a proposed resolution of ratification, which may include reservations, declarations, or understandings; (6) Senate approval of advice and consent to ratification by a two-thirds majority; (7) ratification by the President; (8) deposit of instrument of ratification; and (9) proclamation.

While the House of Representatives does not participate in the treaty-making process, legislation implementing any treaties requires action by both houses of Congress.[1]

Generally, issues related to disability rights have received bipartisan agreement in Congress, and there has been support for CRPD among some Senators from both parties. Many policymakers—including those in the Obama Administration—agree that existing U.S. laws are generally in line with CRPD's provisions, and that no U.S. laws or policies would change as a result of U.S. ratification of the Convention. At the same time, other policymakers contend that ratification of CRPD would adversely affect U.S. sovereignty and interests.

During Senate debates on CRPD ratification, a number of issues were discussed and may continue to be points of contention during the 113th Congress. For example, some policymakers have expressed concern regarding the Convention's possible impact on existing U.S. laws and policies, particularly the role and authority of CRPD's monitoring body, the Committee on the Rights of Persons with Disabilities. (The committee makes non-binding recommendations and has no authority over U.S. law.) Senators may also debate the potential benefits to U.S. ratification, such as the ability of the United States to advocate and share its experiences regarding the rights of disabled persons in global fora, and improved disability rights for U.S. citizens living and traveling abroad.

Another key area of debate includes the impact of U.S. ratification, if any, on parental rights, particularly regarding decisions related to the education of disabled children. Some policymakers have also raised questions about CRPD's possible impact on healthcare—including the extent to which, if any, the Convention addresses existing laws and policies related to abortion.[3]

OBJECTIVES AND STRUCTURE

The CRPD and its Optional Protocol were adopted by the U.N. General Assembly in December 2006.[4] The treaty was opened for signature on March 30, 2007, and entered into force on May 3, 2008.

Many experts view CRPD's adoption as the culmination of a gradual shift in international perceptions toward persons with disabilities from "objects" of charity, medical treatment, and social protection to "subjects" with fundamental rights who are able to make life decisions based on free and informed consent and as active members of society.[5]

The overall purpose of CRPD is to promote, protect, and ensure the full and equal enjoyment of all human rights and fundamental freedoms by all persons with disabilities.

Parties to the treaty agree to "undertake to ensure and promote the full realization of all human rights and fundamental freedoms for all persons with disabilities without discrimination of any kind on the basis of disability."[6]

CRPD Timeline: Key Dates

2002-2006: The Convention text was negotiated during eight sessions of an Ad Hoc Committee of the U.N. General Assembly. The United States observed and/or participated in these sessions.

December 2006: CRPD was adopted as General Assembly resolution 66/229. The Bush Administration joined the consensus adopting the resolution, but indicated it would not sign or ratify the treaty due to concerns over U.S. sovereignty.

March 2007: CRPD was opened for signature. May 2008: CRPD entered into force.

July 2009: President Barack Obama signed CRPD on behalf of the United States, stating that it would benefit disabled persons worldwide, including U.S. citizens.

May 2012: The President transmitted CRPD to the Senate for advice and consent to ratification, where it was received and referred to SFRC.

July 2012: SFRC reported CRPD favorably to the full Senate by a vote of 13 in favor and 6 against, subject to three reservations, eight understandings, and two declarations.

December 2012: The full Senate voted against providing advice and consent to ratification of CRPD by a vote of 61 to 38.

The Convention sets broad goals of autonomy, equality, acceptance, and accessibility for individuals with disabilities. It does not provide a definition of "disability." It acknowledges that the term is an "evolving concept" that results from "the interaction between persons with impairments and attitudinal and environmental barriers that hinders full and effective participation in society on an equal basis with others." (For example, a person in a wheelchair might fail to gain employment not because he or she uses a wheelchair, but because environmental barriers—such as stairs, lack of ramps, or insufficient transportation—impede access to the work place.)

Parties to CRPD agree to take appropriate measures to carry out a range of policies, laws, and administrative measures. The Convention's provisions can grouped into five general themes:

- **Equality and non-discrimination**—CRPD prohibits discrimination and requires States Parties to recognize that "all persons are equal before and under the law and are entitled without any discrimination to the equal protection and equal benefit of the law."[7]Accordingly, States Parties are required to take steps to ensure that reasonable accommodations are provided to persons with disabilities.[8]
- **Accessibility and personal mobility**—States Parties must take measures to ensure that persons with disabilities have equal access to the physical environment, to transportation, to information and communications, and to other facilities open or provided to the public.[9] States Parties also must ensure "liberty of movement" and freedom of disabled persons to choose their nationality and residence on an equal basis with others.
- **Education**—States Parties are required to "ensure an inclusive education system at all levels."[10] Persons with disabilities must be offered the same opportunities for free primary and secondary education as others in their communities, and their individual requirements must be reasonably accommodated. Within the general education system, persons with disabilities shall receive the support required "to facilitate their effective education."[11]
- **Work and employment**—CRPD recognizes the right of disabled persons to work on an equal basis with others in an environment that is "open, inclusive and accessible to persons with disabilities."[12] Parties agree to prohibit employee discrimination against disabled persons and, if necessary, to adopt laws barring such discrimination in the employment process, including recruitment, hiring, retention, promotion, and termination.[13]
- **Health**—The Convention calls on States Parties to ensure that persons with disabilities have equal access to the same range, quality, and standard of free or affordable health care and programs as provided to other persons—including in the areas of sexual and reproductive

health.[14] Under the Convention, health care professionals must provide equal care to persons with disabilities.

CRPD offers other broad legal protections, such as ensuring that persons with disabilities are not deprived of liberty, either unlawfully or arbitrarily.[15] In addition, States Parties are required to take measures to protect disabled persons from exploitation and violence and abuse, as well as in emergency situations such as armed conflict, humanitarian crises, and natural disasters. States Parties must also take steps to ensure that persons with disabilities are able to attain and maintain maximum independence through comprehensive habilitation and rehabilitation services. Parties must also guarantee equal political rights for disabled persons, including voting protection and political participation.

Selected Activities Undertaken by States Parties to CRPD

An August 2012 report on the status of CRPD by U.N. Secretary-General Ban Ki-moon highlighted States Parties' efforts to implement the Convention's provisions.[16] For example,

- Brazil established a National Human Rights Office under the Office of the President to monitor CRPD's implementation;
- Indonesia is implementing a national plan of action on persons with disabilities for 2004-2013;
- Mexico adopted a general law in May 2011 on the social inclusion of persons with disabilities, and launched a national mechanism to implement and monitor national policies and actions plans for the rights of persons with disabilities;
- Paraguay adopted a law that requires public institutions to reserve at least 5% of staff positions for persons with disabilities;
- Spain approved a regulation regarding basic conditions for the participation of persons with disabilities in the political and electoral process; and
- Qatar launched a national development strategy that included social protections for persons with disabilities, and in 2010 introduced a national population strategy that focused on empowering persons with disabilities through anti-discrimination and equal opportunity measures.

Optional Protocol

The Optional Protocol to the CRPD establishes two procedures aimed at strengthening implementation and monitoring of the Convention.[17] The first is an individual communications procedure that allows individuals or groups of individuals from States Parties to bring petitions to the committee claiming breaches of their rights. The second is an inquiry procedure that authorizes the committee to undertake inquiries of grave or systematic violations of the Convention. The Optional Protocol, which entered into force on May 3, 2008, has been signed by 91 countries and ratified or acceded to by 76 countries. The United States has not signed or ratified the Optional Protocol.

Conference of States Parties

Under Article 40 of CRPD, the Conference of States Parties—composed of States Parties to the Convention—has the authority to consider any matter with regard to implementation of the Convention. The Conference has met four times since CRPD entered into force in 2008. Participants have discussed issues ranging from accessibility and reasonable accommodation to CRPD's role in achieving the Millennium Development Goals.[18] The fifth Conference session was held in New York from September 12 to 14, 2012, and featured the theme, "Making the CRPD Count for Women and Children."

Committee on the Rights of Persons with Disabilities

The Committee on the Rights of Persons with Disabilities, established under Article 34 of CRPD, is the monitoring body of the Convention. It is composed of 18 independent experts elected by the Conference of States Parties, taking into account geographic distribution. States Parties are required to submit periodic reports to the committee on their implementation of CRPD, including an initial report within the first two years of ratification or accession and regular reports every four years. The committee examines each report and makes suggestions and general recommendations to the concerned States Parties. Under the CRPD Optional Protocol, the committee may examine individual complaints regarding alleged violation of the Convention by States Parties to the Protocol. The committee meets about twice a year in Geneva, and to date has held eight sessions. The ninth session will be held from April

15 to 19, 2013, when the committee expects to consider reports from Australia, Austria, El Salvador, and Paraguay.[19]

OBAMA ADMINISTRATION ACTIONS

On July 30, 2009, President Obama signed the Convention. The Administration transmitted it to the Senate for advice and consent to ratification on May 17, 2012, where it was received, referred to the Committee on Foreign Relations (SFRC), and placed on the committee calendar. In his letter of transmittal, the President expressed his support for U.S. ratification of CRPD, stating that it would "position the United States to occupy the global leadership role to which our domestic record already attests."[20] The Administration proposed three reservations, five understandings, and one declaration to accompany the treaty:

Reservations, Understandings, and Declarations that may Accompany U.S. Ratification of Treaties

The Senate Committee on Foreign Relations may recommend that the Senate approve a treaty conditionally, granting its advice and consent subject to certain stipulations that the President must accept before proceeding to ratification. These stipulations are generally referred to as "Reservations, Understandings, and Declarations" (RUDs). The President may also propose RUDs at the time he transmits the treaty to the Senate or during the Senate's consideration of the treaty.

"Reservations" are specific qualifications or stipulations that modify U.S. obligations without necessarily changing the treaty language.

"Understandings" are interpretive statements that clarify or elaborate, rather than change, the provisions of a treaty. They are generally deemed to be consistent with the obligations imposed by the treaty.

"Declarations" are statements of purpose, policy, or position related to matters raised by the treaty in question but not altering or limiting any of its provisions.[22]

- a **federalism reservation**, which states that U.S. obligations under CRPD are limited to those measures appropriate to the federal system, such as the enforcement of the Americans with Disabilities Act;[21]

- a **private conduct reservation**, which states that the United States does not accept CRPD provisions that address private conduct, except as mandated by U.S. law;
- a **torture or cruel, inhuman, or degrading treatment reservation**, which states that persons with disabilities are protected against torture and other degrading treatment consistent with U.S. obligations under the U.N. Convention Against Torture and Other Cruel, Inhuman, or Degrading Treatment or Punishment, and the International Covenant on Civil and Political Rights;
- a **first amendment understanding**, which says that the United States understands that CRPD does not authorize or require actions restricting speech, expression, or association that are protected by the Constitution;
- an **economic, social, and cultural rights understanding**, which says the United States understands that CRPD prevents disability discrimination with respect to economic, social and cultural rights, insofar as such rights are recognized and implemented under U.S. law;
- an **equal employment opportunity understanding**, which states that the United States understands that U.S. law protects disabled persons against unequal pay, and that CRPD does not require the adoption of a comparable framework for persons with disabilities;
- a **uniformed military employee hiring understanding**, which states that the United States does not recognize rights in the Convention that exceed those under U.S. law in regards to military hiring, promotion, and other employment-related issues;
- a **definition of disability understanding**, which states that CRPD does not define "disability" or "persons with disabilities," and that the United States understands the definitions of these terms to be consistent with U.S. law;[23] and
- a **non-self executing declaration**, which states that no new laws would be required as a result of U.S. ratification of CRPD.

The federalism reservation and non-self executing declaration are standard RUDs that have accompanied nearly every treaty transmitted to the Senate by the President in modern times. Policymakers have also proposed private conduct reservations for several human rights treaties because of the potential impact on the private lives of U.S. citizens. Other RUDs proposed by the

Administration, including the understanding addressing the definition of disability, are tailored to specific CRPD provisions.

The Obama Administration's support for the Convention is a marked departure from President George W. Bush's policy toward the Convention. During CRPD negotiations between 2003 and 2006, the Bush Administration indicated that because disability issues were in the purview of domestic policy and law, "the United States had no intention of becoming party to the treaty."[24] The Bush Administration did, however join consensus on the General Assembly resolution that adopted the treaty and opened it for signature.[25] Neither President Bush nor President Obama signed, or indicated intent to sign, the Convention's Optional Protocol.

SENATE ACTIONS

On July 31, 2012, the Senate Foreign Relations Committee (SFRC) reported CRPD favorably to the full Senate by a vote of 13 in favor and 6 against.[26] To address the concerns of some opponents, the committee agreed to the following understandings and declarations (in addition to or modifying the aforementioned RUDs proposed by President Obama):

- a **role of the Disabilities Committee understanding**, which states that the committee has no authority to compel actions by States Parties, and that the United States does not consider the conclusions, recommendations, or general comments issued by the committee as constituting customary international law or to be legally binding in the United States in any manner;
- an **abortion-related understanding**, which states that nothing in the agreement requires States Parties to provide any health program or procedure; rather, the Convention requires parties to provide health programs and procedures to individuals with disabilities on a non-discriminatory basis;
- a **best interests of the child understanding**, which states that the use of "best interests of the child" in CRPD Article 7(2) will be applied and interpreted as it is under U.S. law, and that nothing in Article 7 requires a change to existing U.S. law;[29]
- a **definitions understanding** that modifies President Obama's proposed understanding on the definition of disability—it clarifies that the terms "disability," "persons with disabilities," "undue burden"

(terms not defined by the CRPD), "discrimination on the basis of disability," and "reasonable accommodation," are defined in U.S law; and

- a **U.S. obligations declaration**, which states that current U.S. law fulfills or exceeds the obligations of the Convention.[30]

On December 4, 2012, the Senate voted against providing advice and consent to ratification of CRPD by a vote of 61 to 38. With a few exceptions, the vote was split along party lines: 55 Democrats and 6 Republicans voted in favor of the treaty, and 38 Republicans voted against it. At the adjournment of the 112th Congress, CRPD was returned to SFRC in accordance with Senate rules. Majority Leader Harry Reid stated that if the treaty were voted favorably out of SFRC during the 113th Congress, he planned to bring CRPD "up for a vote" in the Senate.[31]

Consideration of Other Treaties

During the 113th Congress, the Senate may consider several other treaties, such as the U.N. Convention on the Law of the Sea, the U.N. Convention on the Elimination of All Forms of Discrimination Against Women (CEDAW), and the U.N. Convention on the Rights of the Child (CRC). Similarly to CRPD, these treaties have garnered considerable attention from policymakers and members of the public due to concerns that they could undermine national sovereignty.[27]

The Obama Administration has recommended the U.N. Convention on the Law of the Sea and CEDAW as treaties on which it supports Senate action at this time.[28] CRC has not been transmitted to the Senate by the President for advice and consent to ratification.

During hearings and debates leading up to the votes in SFRC and the full Senate, Senators focused on the Convention's possible impact on U.S. sovereignty, particularly the impact of the recommendations of the Disabilities Committee on domestic laws and policies, as well as the potential effect U.S. ratification might have on existing U.S. abortion laws. Some Members also argued that treaties should not be considered during a lame duck session of Congress. Thirty-six Senators signed a letter to Majority Leader Reid and Minority Leader Mitch McConnell stating that Members of the 113th Congress should be "afforded the opportunity to review and consider any international agreements that are outstanding at the time of their election."[32] Opponents of this position noted that since the 1970s, the Senate has provided its advice and consent to ratification of treaties 19 times during lame duck sessions.[33]

U.S. Laws Protecting the Rights of Individuals with Disabilities[34]

The U.N. Convention on the Rights of Persons with Disabilities requires States Parties to adopt "all appropriate legislative, administrative and other measures" to implement its provisions.[35] As previously discussed, CRPD sets forth obligations for States Parties in a range of contexts, including accessibility, education, employment, equal rights, and health. The language of the Convention is broad and generally does not provide specific standards or requirements.[36] State Parties must thus consider whether existing laws satisfy CRPD requirements or whether new measures may be required for compliance.

Generally, many U.S. policymakers agree that existing U.S. laws and policies are compatible with the Convention. For example, in his letter of transmittal to the Senate, President Obama stated that existing U.S. law is "consistent with and sufficient to implement the Convention, including the Americans with Disabilities Act (ADA), the Rehabilitation Act, and the Individuals with Disabilities Education Act (IDEA)." In addition, SFRC adopted, by a vote of 14 in favor and 5 against, a declaration to accompany CRPD which states that "current United States law fulfills or exceeds the obligations of the convention for the United States."[37]

In its executive report, SFRC also noted that "[t]he United States has a comprehensive network of existing federal and state disability laws and enforcement mechanisms" and that "[i]n the large majority of cases, existing federal and state law meets or exceeds the requirements of the Convention."[38]

Indeed, the United States historically has recognized the rights of individuals with disabilities through various constitutional and statutory protections, including the Americans with Disabilities Act of 1990 (ADA).[39] As such, many of the Convention's provisions addressing the protection of disability rights already exist in federal law. In fact, some CRPD requirements appear to be modeled after these U.S. disability laws.[40]

Federal versus State Law

It is important to note that some of the obligations in the Convention address matters typically covered by U.S. state laws, such as guardianship, civil commitment, and education.[41] As discussed earlier, to address concerns regarding constitutional principles of federalism, the Obama Administration proposed, and SFRC adopted, a federalism reservation to CRPD, stating,

> This Convention shall be implemented by the Federal Government of the United States of America to the extent that it exercises legislative and judicial jurisdiction over the matters covered therein, and otherwise by the state and local governments; to the extent that state and local governments exercise jurisdiction over such matters, the obligations of the United States of America under the Convention are limited to the Federal Government's taking measures appropriate to the Federal system, which may include enforcement action against state and local actions that are inconsistent with the Constitution, the Americans with Disabilities Act, or other Federal laws, with the ultimate objective of fully implementing the Convention.[42]

Thus, the authority of state and local governments would not be controlled by the terms of the treaty unless they are acting subject to federal law. For example, education is an issue that generally falls under state and local jurisdiction. However, the federal government has enacted legislation requiring schools that receive federal funding to implement certain federal standards.[43] If the United States were to ratify the Convention, the federal legislation must comport with the obligations imposed by the Convention, but state and local policies on education that are not implicated by the federal legislation—for example, homeschooling—would not be governed by the Convention's provisions.

Existing Laws and Policies

The following sections discuss the most significant existing U.S. laws that might fulfill the requirements of the CRPD, if the Senate provides its advice and consent to ratification. A number of other disability laws are in effect that may likewise satisfy obligations required by the Convention. Many of these are discussed specifically in both the President's transmittal package and the SFRC Committee Report on the CRPD.[44]

U.S. Constitution

Many of the rights required by CRPD are already guaranteed by the U.S. Constitution, particularly the CRPD provisions relating to equal rights and equal access to justice systems.[45] For instance, the Equal Protection Clause of the Fourteenth Amendment prevents U.S. states from denying any person under its jurisdiction "the equal protection of the laws."[46] This constitutional requirement for equal protection under the law is applicable to the federal government through the Due Process Clause of the Fifth Amendment, which provides that "[n]o person ... shall be deprived of life, liberty, or property without due process of the law."

Courts therefore have construed laws that discriminate against people with disabilities as unconstitutional when there is no rational basis or legitimate purpose for those laws. In *City of Cleburne v. Cleburne Living Center, Inc.*, for example, the U.S. Supreme Court determined that a city ordinance requiring a special use permit for the operation of a group home for the mentally disabled was unconstitutional.[47] The Court interpreted the Equal Protection Clause as a "direction that all persons similarly situated should be treated alike," ultimately concluding that "requiring the permit in this case appears to us to rest on an irrational prejudice against the mentally retarded."[48] In sum, as the President observed in his transmittal package to the Senate, the Fifth and Fourteenth Amendments of the Constitution ensure that all individuals are equal before the law.

In addition, the Eighth Amendment of the Constitution, which is applicable to the federal government and to states through the Due Process Clause of the Fourteenth Amendment, bars the use of "cruel and unusual punishment."[49] In general, punishments violate this amendment when they are "grossly disproportionate" to the crime committed.[50] The Supreme Court has held that deliberate indifference to prisoners' serious medical needs, including the requirements of disabled inmates, would constitute cruel and unusual punishment.[51]

Americans with Disabilities Act (ADA)

Enacted in 1990, the Americans with Disabilities Act (ADA) provides broad non-discrimination protections for people with disabilities. As the most comprehensive disability rights law in the United States, the ADA might fulfill many of the CRPD obligations addressing accessibility, employment, transportation, health care, and equal participation in government and private programs.[52]

The ADA received bipartisan support, as did the ADA Amendments Act in 2008.[53] Among other changes, the 2008 amendments broadened the definition of disability to expand coverage to a wider range of individuals with disabilities. Currently, the ADA defines disability as "(A) a physical or mental impairment that substantially limits one or more of the major life activities of such individual; (B) a record of such an impairment; or (C) being regarded as having such an impairment."[54] The act also contains rules of construction providing, among other things, that the definition of disability shall be construed in favor of broad coverage to the maximum extent permitted by the terms of the law.[55]

Although the Convention does not define disability, it does identify which individuals may qualify as persons with disabilities, including "those who have long-term physical, mental, intellectual or sensory impairments which in interaction with various barriers may hinder their full and effective participation in society on an equal basis with others."[56] During negotiations for the Convention, an explicit definition for disability was intentionally omitted so that the term could be altered "depending on the prevailing environment from society to society."[57] As previously discussed, to clarify the U.S. position on how disability would be defined under the Convention, the Administration proposed, and SFRC adopted, an understanding stating that the term will be defined coextensively with its definitions under domestic law.[58]

Employment

The ADA provides protections related to employment of individuals with disabilities. Employment discrimination protections under the ADA apply to employers with 15 or more employees[59] and to state and local governments.[60] The ADA generally prohibits discrimination in employment based on an individual's disability if the individual is otherwise qualified for the position.[61] Discrimination based on a disability is prohibited across a range of employment decisions, including application procedures; hiring, retention, and promotion; compensation; training; and other terms of employment.[62] The ADA requires that employers offer qualified individuals reasonable accommodation to perform the desired position if such an accommodation would not create an undue hardship on the employer's business.[63]

Under the ADA, *reasonable accommodation* may include making facilities readily accessible to individuals with disabilities; offering alternative work schedules; reassignment to a different position; modification of equipment; assistance with communications needs; or other similar accommodations.[64] *Undue hardship* is defined as "an action requiring significant difficulty or expense."[65] To determine whether an accommodation constitutes an undue hardship, an employer may consider its nature and cost; the financial resources involved and the accommodation's impact on expenses and resources; and the type of operation of the employer and its facilities.[66]

State and Local Governments

Title II of the ADA provides that no qualified individual with a disability shall be excluded from participation in or be denied the benefits of the services, programs, or activities of a public entity or be subjected to discrimination by any such entity.[67] "Public entity" is defined as state and local governments, any department or other instrumentality of a state or local government, and certain transportation authorities.

In *Olmstead v. L.C.*, the Supreme Court interpreted Title II of the ADA to find that individuals with mental disabilities have the right to live in the community rather than in institutions if "the State's treatment professionals have determined that community placement is appropriate, the transfer from institutional care to a less restrictive setting is not opposed by the affected individual, and the placement can be reasonably accommodated, taking into account the resources available to the State and the needs of others with mental disabilities."[68] In other words, the ADA's prohibitions on discrimination by state and local governments may require the placement of persons with mental disabilities in community settings rather than institutions. The Court found that "[u]njustified isolation ... is properly regarded as discrimination based on disability."[69]

Public Accommodations

Title III of the ADA provides that no individual shall be discriminated against on the basis of disability in the full and equal enjoyment of the goods, services, facilities, privileges, advantages, or accommodations of any place of public accommodation by any person who owns, leases (or leases to), or operates a place of public accommodation.[70] Entities that are covered by the term "public accommodation" are listed, and include, among others, hotels, restaurants, theaters, auditoriums, laundromats, travel services, museums, parks, zoos, private schools, day care centers, professional offices of health care providers, and gymnasiums.[71] Religious institutions or entities controlled by religious institutions are not included on the list.

There are some limitations on the non-discrimination requirements, and a failure to remove architectural barriers is not a violation unless such a removal is "readily achievable."[72] "Readily achievable" is defined as meaning "easily accomplishable and able to be carried out without much difficulty or expense."[73] Reasonable modifications in practices, policies, or procedures are required unless they would fundamentally alter the nature of the goods, services, facilities, or privileges or they would result in an undue burden.[74] As previously discussed, an undue burden is defined as an action involving "significant difficulty or expense."[75]

Rehabilitation Act of 1973

While the ADA prohibits discrimination against individuals based on disability by state and local governments and certain private entities, Section 504 of the Rehabilitation Act of 1973[76] provides similar protection in the context of federal entities and federal programs. It provides that

> [n]o otherwise qualified individual with a disability in the United States ... shall, solely by reason of her or his disability, be excluded from the participation in, be denied the benefits of, or be subjected to discrimination under any program or activity receiving Federal financial assistance or under any program or activity conducted by any Executive agency or by the United States Postal Service.[77]

Each federal agency is then required to promulgate regulations implementing the act.[78]

The standards for establishing a violation of Section 504 of the Rehabilitation Act and the ADA are essentially the same. Furthermore, the Rehabilitation Act explicitly adopts the same requirements and standards as the ADA in cases alleging employment discrimination based on disability (for example, reasonable accommodations required unless such accommodations would create an undue hardship).[79]

Individuals with Disabilities Education Act (IDEA)

The Individuals with Disabilities Education Act (IDEA) is the major federal statute for the education of children with disabilities.[80] As a result, it might satisfy the education provisions in the CRPD.[81]

IDEA authorizes federal funding for special education and related services and, for states that accept these funds, it sets out principles under which special education and related services are to be provided. It requires that states and school districts make available a "free appropriate public education" (FAPE) to all children with disabilities, generally between the ages of three and 21.[82] FAPE is defined to include "special education and related services that—(A) have been provided at public expense, under public supervision and direction, and without charge; (B) meet the standards of the State educational agency; (C) include an appropriate preschool, elementary school, or secondary school education in the State involved; and (D) are provided in conformity with the individual education program required [under the statute]."[83]

Students receiving special education services under IDEA must have an individual education plan (IEP), which specifies the particular services that will be provided to meet the student's educational needs.[84] After a child has been identified as a child with a disability under IDEA, an individualized education team is formed to write an individualized education program for the child.[85] The IEP must indicate the child's current levels of academic achievement and functional performance; measurable annual goals; the special education and related services to be provided; and the extent to which the child is to be educated with children without disabilities.[86] Additionally, when developing a child's IEP, the IEP team must consider the child's language and communication needs, including whether Braille, sign language, or other assistance would be appropriate.[87]

One of the stated purposes of IDEA is that special education students should be educated with students without disabilities "to the maximum extent possible."[88] IDEA requires that separate schooling or special classes occur "only when the nature or severity of the disability of a child is such that education in regular classes with the use of supplementary aids and services cannot be achieved satisfactorily."[89]

Policy Issues

The question of U.S. ratification of CRPD has generated debate among U.S. policymakers and members of the public. A significant issue underlying almost all aspects of these discussions is the treaty's possible impact on national sovereignty. Opponents of the Convention argue that treaties are the "supreme Law of the Land" under the Constitution, and that U.S. ratification of CRPD could supersede federal, state, and local laws.[90] Specifically, critics are concerned that ratification could lead to the United Nations, the international community, or the Disabilities Committee having authority over existing U.S. laws and policies related to disability rights, as well as the private lives of U.S. citizens in areas such as education, health care, and parental rights.

Supporters of ratification emphasize that CRPD is a non-discrimination treaty that does not create new obligations. They contend that U.S. laws such as the ADA meet, and in some cases exceed, the requirements of the Convention, thereby having little or no impact on U.S. sovereignty. Proponents also note that the RUDs that may accompany the treaty—particularly the non-self executing declaration which states that no new laws would be created as a result of U.S. ratification—address any concerns that the CRPD may undermine national sovereignty. More broadly, supporters point out that many of CRPD's provisions call on States Parties to take "all *appropriate* measures" [emphasis added], thereby leaving it to governments to determine what actions are appropriate based on their domestic laws and policies. More broadly, many emphasize that CRPD brings increased global attention to rights of disabled persons, and that ratification has led some countries to adopt laws and policies to improve disability rights. These and other selected issues are discussed in more detail in the following sections.

The Role of the Disabilities Committee

Opponents of CRPD ratification are concerned about the role of the Disabilities Committee in monitoring States Parties' compliance with CRPD. Specifically, critics are concerned that committee recommendations and decisions could supersede U.S. laws and presume authority affecting the lives, freedoms, and decisions of private citizens. Opponents highlight decisions made by other human rights treaty committees that in their view advocate abortion, undermine parental rights, or make recommendations that extend beyond the scope of the treaty. They are worried that such decisions or recommendations could be used in U.S. courts to challenge existing laws and policies.

Proponents of the CRPD ratification, including the Obama Administration, emphasize that any decisions or recommendations made by the committee are "advisory only" and non-binding under international and domestic law.[91] Supporters also note that there are no established rules in CRPD for enforcing the committee's decisions or addressing treaty non-compliance. Moreover, several human rights treaties ratified by the United States have monitoring committees similar to CRPD, and there appears to be no instance where a U.S. federal court or the executive branch has construed a committee's recommendations or decisions as having the force of law.[92]

To address concerns related to the committee's role and authority, the Senate Foreign Relations Committee (SFRC) adopted an understanding to accompany CRPD, which stated that the committee has no authority to compel action by States Parties, and that the United States does not consider conclusions, recommendations, or general comments issued by the committee as constituting customary international law or to be legally binding on the United States in any manner.[93]

CRPD as an Instrument of U.S. Foreign Policy

Supporters of CRPD contend that U.S. ratification would enhance the United States' credibility as it advocates the rights of persons with disabilities globally. For example, Obama Administration officials state that ratification will put the United States in the best possible position to influence the international community on disability rights, and that non-ratification would make it "difficult" to advance such interests.[94]

Supporters also emphasize that as a leader in disability rights, the United States could work within the framework of CRPD, such as in the Conference of States Parties, to provide expertise, guidance, and technical assistance to countries that seek to improve the well-being of disabled persons, particularly in the areas of education, employment, and accessibility. Moreover, many supporters suggest that, as a State Party, the United States could engage with the Disabilities Committee to nominate and vote for committee experts—including, perhaps, a U.S. citizen—to leverage U.S. expertise and influence the work of the committee.

On the other side, opponents argue that the United States does not need to ratify CRPD to demonstrate its credibility and leadership in disability rights. They suggest that U.S. laws and policies, such as the ADA, are robust examples of U.S. commitment to the issue.

Critics also express concern regarding CRPD provisions that would obligate the United States to report to the treaty's monitoring body, the Disabilities Committee.

Specifically, they worry that instead of providing a forum to share U.S. expertise or advocate disability rights, the committee might be used as a platform for political criticism of the United States, particularly by countries with lesser human rights standards. Opponents also emphasize that U.S. ratification itself may not enhance the rights of disabled persons in countries with poor human rights records. Any such improvements, they argue, can only be made by the governments of these countries.

Possible Impact on U.S. Citizens and Businesses Abroad

When advocating for U.S. ratification of CRPD, many supporters highlight two key benefits for the United States. First, proponents contend that U.S. ratification, as well as the United States' overall support for the treaty, may improve the lives of U.S. citizens with disabilities living, working, or traveling abroad—including students, retirees, veterans, and members of the U.S. Armed Forces. Currently, many developed countries do not have comparable disability services or infrastructure. This makes it difficult for U.S. citizens to be employed, move freely, and have the same rights and access to disability-related services in other countries as they would in the United States.[95] Supporters suggest that as more countries ratify the Convention and implement its provisions, disability rights and services in other countries may improve.

Second, some CRPD supporters maintain that U.S. ratification would help U.S. companies that already comply with higher disability standards. Since the ADA was enacted in 1990, U.S. businesses have been required to make reasonable accommodations for their employees and customers, while businesses in countries with less stringent laws and policies have not been required to do so. Proponents suggest that CRPD ratification by the United States and other countries may lead foreign companies to institute such standards and thus help "level the playing field" for U.S. businesses.[96] In addition, some maintain that increased global standards for and awareness of disabilities rights through CRPD ratification may provide new economic opportunities for U.S. companies. Supporters note that if international disabilities standards were to improve, new markets could emerge for U.S. companies that develop, manufacture, and sell disability-related products and technologies.

The extent to which U.S. ratification of CRPD may positively affect U.S. businesses or disabled U.S. citizens living or traveling abroad is not entirely clear. States Parties to CRPD are responsible for implementing its provisions, and U.S. ratification of the treaty does not guarantee that all countries will fulfill their obligations under the Convention. Ultimately, CRPD's impact on disability rights and on the scope of the global market for disability-related services, expertise, and products will become more apparent as individual countries begin to implement the Convention's provisions.

Potential Impact on Parental Authority

Some opponents of CRPD contend that the treaty undermines the rights of parents of disabled children. Specifically, many take issue with Article 7(2), which states, "In all actions concerning children with disabilities, the best interests of the child shall be a primary consideration." Critics believe that this provision may give governments, and not U.S. parents, the right to make educational and treatment-related decisions for their disabled children. Additionally, opponents are concerned that the Disabilities Committee could have the authority to make decisions regarding the "best interests" of disabled children in the United States. For example, homeschooling advocates worry that the committee could declare homeschooling inconsistent with the best interest of the child, thereby undermining the right of parents to educate their children as they see fit.[97]

Supporters of the Convention, including the Obama Administration, maintain that CRPD would not undermine the rights of U.S. parents. They contend that existing federal, state, and local laws provide adequate protection for parents to do what they believe is in the best interests of their children. These protections, they emphasize, would be ensured through proposed reservations, understandings, and declarations (RUDs) to CRPD that include a non-self executing declaration and private conduct and federalism reservations.[98] To further alleviate concerns about parental rights, SFRC adopted an understanding that states that the use of "best interests of the child" in Article 7(2) will be applied and interpreted as it is under U.S. law, and that nothing in Article 7 requires a change to existing U.S. law.[99] More broadly, some supporters emphasize that concerns about CRPD's potential impact on parental rights should be viewed in the context of other provisions that appear to support the role of parents and families in the lives of disabled children.[100]

Possible Impact on Abortion Laws and Policies

The debate over U.S. ratification of CRPD reflects concern as to whether, and to what extent, the treaty might address abortion. In particular, some critics have raised questions about CRPD Article 25, which states that States Parties shall

a) Provide persons with disabilities with the same range, quality and standard of free or affordable health care and programmes as provided to other persons, including in the area of sexual and reproductive health and population-based public health programmes; [and]

b) Provide those health services needed by persons with disabilities specifically because of their disabilities, including early identification and intervention as appropriate, and services designed to minimize and prevent further disabilities, including among children and older persons....

Many CRPD opponents maintain that abortion is an issue that should be handled at a state or local level, and not by an international body. They are concerned that the term "sexual and reproductive health" could be interpreted to be a euphemism for abortion.[101] They also worry that U.S. ratification could obligate the United States to provide persons with disabilities access to free or affordable abortions or to overturn parental notification laws, thereby undermining current laws that ban federal funding for abortion.[102] When advocating these views, critics note that after CRPD was adopted by the General Assembly, a Bush Administration official remarked that the United States understood that the phrase "reproductive health" in Article 25(a) did not include abortion.[103] They further emphasize that Poland, Malta, and Monaco included reservations or declarations to CRPD that stated that nothing in Article 25 shall be interpreted to include abortion.[104] Some opponents also suggest that the Disabilities Committee could interpret Article 25 to include abortion.

CRPD advocates note that the word "abortion" is never mentioned in the treaty and contend that no U.S laws related to abortion would be created as a result of U.S. ratification. They maintain that references to sexual and reproductive health and health services are non-discrimination requirements that would not obligate the United States to modify its existing abortion laws or other health services. The Obama Administration emphasizes that Article 25, and the treaty as a whole, already complies with obligations under the ADA; specifically, any health care programs and benefits provided under domestic law, including those related to "sexual and reproductive health," should also be provided to disabled persons.[105] Supporters also point out that any recommendations made by the Disabilities Committee related to abortion are not legally binding. As discussed earlier, CRPD has no established mechanisms for treaty non-compliance; it relies primarily on States Parties to fulfill their treaty obligations.

To address ongoing concerns about CRPD's potential impact on existing abortion laws, SFRC approved an understanding stating that nothing in the

Convention, including Article 25, addresses "the provision of any particular health program or procedure."[106] The understanding amended a previous proposal by Senator Marco Rubio that stated that Article 25(a) does not include abortion or create any abortion rights, nor could it be interpreted to constitute the support, endorsement, or promotion of abortion (including as a method of family planning).[107] Although the amended measure was adopted by SFRC, several Senators have expressed dismay that the word "abortion" was not specifically mentioned in the understanding.[108]

Issues on the Horizon

As U.S. policymakers continue to debate U.S. ratification of CRPD and States Parties take steps toward implementing the Convention, Members may wish to monitor several potential issues:

- **Evaluating effectiveness**—CRPD has been in force for nearly five years. As a result, there is minimal evidence demonstrating its effectiveness or potential areas for improvement. Evaluating the country-specific or global impact of the treaty may be particularly difficult because there is a lack of consistent or comparable data on persons with disabilities worldwide and often within countries and regions.
- **Challenges to implementation**—As States Parties take steps toward implementing the treaty's provisions, Senators may wish to monitor any challenges these countries face and how, if at all, CRPD mechanisms such as the Conference of States Parties or Disabilities Committee may assist with such issues. The United States may also consider ways that it can contribute to these bodies and share its expertise in disability rights as a CRPD observer.
- **Role of civil society**—Civil society, including human rights and disability rights groups, play a particularly important role not only in raising awareness of disability issues, but also in holding governments accountable to their CRPD commitments. As such, the United States may wish to monitor and encourage the full participation of civil society in CRPD mechanisms, particularly the Disabilities Committee, which is charged with evaluating reports from States Parties—some of which have weak disability rights standards.

APPENDIX A. STATES PARTIES TO CRPD

Afghanistan*	Dominica*	Malaysia	San Marino*
Albania	Dominican Republic*	Maldives	Saudi Arabia*
Algeria	Ecuador*	Mali*	Senegal
Argentina*	Egypt	Malta*	Serbia*
Armenia	El Salvador*	Mauritania*	Seychelles
Australia*	Estonia*	Mauritius	Sierra Leone
Austria*	Ethiopia	Mexico*	Slovakia*
Azerbaijan*	European Union	Mongolia*	Slovenia*
Bahrain	France*	Montenegro*	South Africa*
Bangladesh*	Gabon	Morocco*	Spain*
Barbados	Germany*	Mozambique*	St. Vincent & Grenadines*
Belgium*	Ghana*	Myanmar	Sudan*
Belize	Greece*	Namibia*	Swaziland*
Benin*	Guatemala *	Nauru	Sweden*
Bolivia*	Guinea*	Nepal*	Syrian Arab Republic*
Bosnia and Herzegovina*	Haiti*	New Zealand	Thailand
Brazil*	Honduras*	Nicaragua*	The former Yugoslav
			Republic of Macedonia*
Bulgaria	Hungary*	Niger*	Togo*
Burkina Faso*	India	Nigeria*	Tunisia*
Cambodia	Indonesia	Oman	Turkey
Canada	Israel	Pakistan	Turkmenistan*
Cape Verde	Iran	Panama*	Uganda*
Chile*	Italy*	Paraguay*	Ukraine*
China	Jamaica	Peru*	United Arab Emirates
Colombia	Jordan	Philippines	United Kingdom*
Cook Islands*	Kenya	Portugal*	United Republic of Tanzania*
Costa Rica*	Lao People's Democratic	Poland	Uruguay*
	Republic		
Croatia*	Latvia*	Qatar	Vanuatu
Cuba	Lesotho	Republic of Korea	Yemen*
Cyprus*	Liberia	Republic of Moldova	Zambia
Czech Republic	Lithuania*	Romania	
Denmark	Luxembourg*	Russian Federation	
Djibouti*	Malawi	Rwanda*	

Source: U.N. Treaty Collection.

Note: An asterisk* indicates that the country is a State Party to the CRPD Optional Protocol.

APPENDIX B. KEY CRPD LEGISLATIVE ACTIONS

- **May 17, 2012**: CRPD was received in the Senate and referred to the Committee on Foreign Relations (SFRC) by unanimous consent.
- **July 12, 2012**: SFRC held a hearing, "Convention on the Rights of Persons with Disabilities, Treaty Doc. 112-7."
- **July 26, 2012**: SFRC ordered CRPD to be reported favorably by a vote of 13 in favor and 6 against, with amendments. (See S. Ex.Rept. 112-6.)
- **July 31, 2012**: CRPD was reported favorably by Senator Kerry, Chairperson of SFRC, with minority views. A resolution of advice and consent to ratification was filed with three reservations, eight understandings, and two declarations.
- **November 27, 2012**: Senators approved a motion to proceed to executive session to consider the treaty in the full Senate by a vote of 61 in favor and 35 against. (See record vote number 205.)
- **November 30, 2012**: The Senate agreed, by unanimous consent, to debate and vote on CRPD on December 4, 2012.
- **December 4, 2012**: The resolution of advice and consent to ratification was not agreed to in the Senate by a vote of 61 in favor and 38 against. (See record vote number 219.)
- **January 3, 2013**: At the adjournment of the 112th Congress, CRPD was automatically returned to SFRC under Rule XXX, Section 2, of the Standing Rules of the Senate.[109]

End Notes

[1] For more information, see U.S. Congress, Senate Committee on Foreign Relations, *Treaties and Other International Agreements: The Role of the United States Senate*, committee print, prepared by the Congressional Research Service, 106th Cong., 2nd sess., January 2001, S. Prt. 106-71 (Washington: GPO, 2001). Also see CRS Report 98-384, *Senate Consideration of Treaties*, by Valerie Heitshusen.

[2] For more information on these conditions, see sections on "Obama Administration Actions" and "Senate Action."

[3] For further discussion of these and other subjects, see the "Policy Issues" section.

[4] U.N. General Assembly Resolution 66/229, adopted December 13, 2006. The Convention was negotiated during eight sessions of an Ad Hoc Committee of the General Assembly from 2002-2006. The negotiating history of the Ad Hoc Committee is available at http://www.un.org/disabilities/default.asp?id=1423. For information on the U.S. position, see the "Obama Administration Actions" section.

[5] Drawn from "United Nations (U.N.) Enable: Convention on the Rights of Persons with Disabilities," at http://www.un.org/disabilities/default.asp?navid=14&pid=150. For additional information on the history of the Convention and U.N. efforts to address disability issues, see "U.N. Enable: History of the United Nations and Disability" at http://www.un.org/disabilities/default.asp?id=121.

[6] CRPD, Article (art.) 4(1).

[7] CRPD, art. 5.

[8] CRPD, art. 10. CRPD also reaffirms that every human being has the "inherent right to life and its effective enjoyment by persons with disabilities on a equal basis with others." It further states that Parties must provide equal access to justice systems and prevent abuse in accordance with international human right laws. The Convention also recognizes the rights of women and children with disabilities.

[9] CPRD, art. 9.

[10] CRPD, art. 24.

[11] Ibid. CRPD also requires Parties to facilitate the use of sign language, Braille, and other modes of communication to assist students with disabilities in fully participating in the educational process.

[12] CRPD, art. 27. Under art. 27, employees with disabilities must also be reasonably accommodated and have access to training and union benefits.

[13] Ibid.

[14] CRPD, art. 25.

[15] For a detailed account of how these provisions apply to U.S. laws and policies, see the "U.S. Laws Protecting the Rights of Individuals with Disabilities" section.

[16] U.N. document A/67/281, *Status of the Convention on the Rights of Persons with Disabilities and the Optional Protocol thereto—Report of the Secretary-General*, August 9, 2012.

[17] Optional Protocols sometimes accompany treaties. They are stand-alone agreements that can be signed and ratified by countries that are not party to the main treaty.

[18] The Millennium Development Goals are a group of measurable development targets agreed to by 189 U.N. member states, including the United States, as part of the 2000 Millennium Declaration. Examples include eradicating extreme hunger and poverty; achieving universal primary education; and reducing child and maternal mortality rates.

[19] For more information on committee procedures, membership, and sessions, see http://www.ohchr.org/en/hrbodies/ crpd/pages/crpdindex.aspx. The committee's monitoring role is further discussed in the "The Role of the Disabilities Committee" section.

[20] U.S. Congress, Senate Committee on Foreign Relations, *Convention on the Rights of Persons with Disabilities*, Message from the President of the United States Transmitting The Convention on the Rights of Persons With Disabilities, Adopted by the United Nations General Assembly on December 13, 2006, and Signed by the United States of America on June 30, 2009, prepared by Office of the President, 112th Congress, 2nd session, May 17, 2012, Treaty Doc. 112-7 (Washington: GPO, 2012) (hereinafter *Treaty Doc. 112-7*).

[21] For a more detailed discussion of the federalism reservation, see the "U.S. Laws Protecting the Rights of Individuals with Disabilities" section. For more information on the ADA, see CRS Report 98-921, *The Americans with Disabilities Act (ADA): Statutory Language and Recent Issues*, by Cynthia Brougher and James V. DeBergh.

[22] Drawn in part from U.S. Congress, Senate Committee on Foreign Relations, *Treaties and Other International Agreements: The Role of the United States Senate*, committee print, prepared by the Congressional Research Service, 106th Cong., 2nd sess., January 2001, S. Prt. 106-71 (Washington: GPO, 2001).

[23] For further discussion of the disability understanding, see the "Senate Action" and "U.S. Laws Protecting the Rights of Individuals with Disabilities" sections.

[24] Department of State, "U.S. Participation in the United Nations, 2005," pp. 68-69. For more information on the Bush Administration position on CRPD, also see, "U.S. Participation in the United Nations, 2006," pp. 79-80.

[25] Statement by Ambassador Richard T. Miller, "Explanation of Position on the Convention on the Rights of Persons with Disabilities, Agenda Item 67(b), in the General Assembly," U.S. Mission to the United Nations Press Release #396(06), December 13, 2006.

[26] U.S. Congress, Senate Committee on Foreign Relations, *Convention on the Rights of Persons with Disabilities (Treaty Doc. 112-7)*, Report Together With Minority Views [To accompany Treaty Doc. 112-7], 112th Cong., 2nd sess., July 31, 2012, Exec. Rept. 112-6 (Washington: GPO, 2012). (Hereinafter referred to as *Senate Exec. Rept. 112-6.*) See Appendix B for a list of all legislative actions related to CRPD.

[27] For more information on CRC and CEDAW, see CRS Report R40484, *The United Nations Convention on the Rights of the Child: Background and Policy Issues*, and CRS Report R40750, *The U.N. Convention on the Elimination of All Forms of Discrimination Against Women (CEDAW): Issues in the U.S. Ratification Debate*, both by Luisa Blanchfield.

[28] Letter from David S. Adams, Assistant Secretary for Legislative Affairs, State Department, to Senator John Kerry, SFRC Chairperson, October 5, 2011.

[29] For a further discussion of this issue, see the "Potential Impact on Parental Authority" section.

[30] For a full list of RUDs approved by SFRC, see *Senate Exec. Rept. 112-6,* pp. 12-14.

[31] Ramsey Cox, "Reid Vows to Take up Disability Treaty in the Next Congress," *The Hill*, December 4, 2012.

[32] Letter to Senator Reid and Senator McConnell, dated September 20, 2012, signed by 36 Republican Senators. All but one of the letter's signatories, then-Senator Scott Brown, voted against CRPD. For more information on lame duck sessions, see CRS Report RL33677, *Lame Duck Sessions of Congress, 1935-2010 (74th-111th Congresses)*, by Richard S. Beth and Jessica Tollestrup.

[33] Senator John Kerry, "Executive Session, Convention on the Rights of Persons with Disabilities," Senate debate, *Congressional Record*, daily edition, December 4, 2012, p. S7378; Ramsey Cox, "Senate rejected United Nations Treaty for Disabled Rights in a 61-38 vote," *The Hill*, December 4, 2012.

[34] This section was written by Cynthia Brougher, Legislative Attorney, and James V. DeBergh, Legislative Attorney.

[35] CRPD, art. 4(a).

[36] For example, the Convention directs States Parties to "take appropriate measures to ensure persons with disabilities access, on an equal basis with others," to various facilities and services. *See* CRPD, art. 9.1. The Convention does not indicate what those measures might be, nor what the standard of accessibility is. Rather, it requires only that whatever facilities or services are provided to individuals without disabilities are also accessible to individuals with disabilities.

[37] *Senate Exec. Rept. 112-6,* p. 14.

[38] Ibid., 6.

[39] 42 U.S.C. §12101 *et seq*.

[40] *Compare* 20 U.S.C. §1400 et seq. *with* CRPD, art. 24.

[41] *Senate Exec. Rept. 112-6,* p. 134.

[42] *Senate Exec. Rept. 112-6,* pp. 14-15.

[43] *See, e.g.*, Individuals with Disabilities Education Act, 20 U.S.C. §1400 *et seq*.

[44] See *Treaty Doc. 112-7*, and *Senate Exec. Rept.* 112-6.
[45] *See, e.g.*, CRPD, art 5, art. 10, art. 13, art. 12, art. 14, art. 15.
[46] U.S. CONST. amend. XIV.
[47] *See* 473 U.S. 432 (1985).
[48] *Id.* at 439, 450.
[49] U.S. CONST. amend. VIII.
[50] *See* Graham v. Florida, 130 S.Ct. 2011 (2010) (citing Harmellin v. Michigan, 501 U.S. 277, 997, 1000-1001 (1991) (Kennedy, J. concurring in part and concurring in judgment)).
[51] *See* Estelle v. Gamble, 429 U.S. 97 (1976).
[52] *See, e.g.*, CRPD, art. 1, art. 5, art. 9, art. 10, art. 18, art. 19, art. 21, art. 25, art. 27, art. 30.
[53] *See* P.L. 110-325, 122 Stat. 3553 (September 25, 2008).
[54] 42 U.S.C. §12102(1).
[55] 42 U.S.C. §12102(4).
[56] CRPD, art. 1.
[57] *See* United Nations Enable, "Are the terms 'disability' and 'persons with disabilities' defined in the Convention?" Frequently Asked Questions Regarding the Convention on the Rights of Persons with Disabilities, available at http://www.un.org/disabilities/default.asp?navid=24&pid=151#sqc3. See also *Treaty Doc. 112-7*, pp. 4-7.
[58] *Senate Exec. Rept. 112-6,* p. 16.
[59] 42 U.S.C. §12111(5)(A).
[60] 42 U.S.C. §12131.
[61] 42 U.S.C. §12112.
[62] 42 U.S.C. §12112(a).
[63] *See* 42 U.S.C. §12112(b)(5).
[64] 42 U.S.C. §12111(9).
[65] 42 U.S.C. §12111(10)(A).
[66] 42 U.S.C. §12111(10)(B).
[67] 42 U.S.C. §§12131-12133.
[68] 527 U.S. 581, 587 (1999).
[69] *Id.* at 597.
[70] 42 U.S.C. §12182.
[71] 42 U.S.C. §12181.
[72] 42 U.S.C. §12182(b)(2)(A)(iv).
[73] 42 U.S.C. §12181.
[74] 42 U.S.C. §12182(b)(2)(A).
[75] 28 C.F.R. §36.104.
[76] 29 U.S.C. §794 (P.L. 93-112, 87 Stat. 355 (September 26, 1973)).
[77] 29 U.S.C.A. §794(a).
[78] *See id.*
[79] *See* 29 U.S.C. §794(d).
[80] 20 U.S.C. §1400 et seq.
[81] *See, e.g.*, CRPD, art. 24.
[82] 20 U.S.C. §1412.
[83] 20 U.S.C. §1401(9).
[84] *See* 20 U.S.C. §1414.
[85] *Id.*
[86] 20 U.S.C. §1414(d)(1)(A).
[87] 20 U.S.C. §1414(d)(3)(B).

[88] 20 U.S.C. §1400.

[89] 20 U.S.C. §1412(a)(5)(A).

[90] U.S. CONST. art. 6. For additional discussion of this issue, see Martin S. Flaherty, "History Right?: Historical Scholarship, Original Understanding, and Treaties as "Supreme Law of the Land," *Columbia Law Review*, Vol. 99, No. 8, December 1999, pp. 2095-2153.

[91] Under art. 36 of CRPD, the committee "considers" States Parties' reports on treaty implementation and "shall make such suggestions and general recommendations" to the State Party.

[92] These include the International Covenant on Civil and Political Rights, and the International Convention on the Elimination of All Forms of Racial Discrimination.

[93] The understanding, which was introduced by Senator John Kerry as an amendment to an amendment proposed by Senator Rubio, was agreed to by a voice vote. The full text is available in *Senate Exec. Rept. 112-6*, p. 16.

[94] Statement of Honorable Judith Heumann, Special Adviser for International Disability Rights, U.S. Department of State, Washington DC, at SFRC Hearing, "Convention on the Rights of Persons with Disabilities (Treaty Doc. 112-7)," July 12, 2012.

[95] A number of veterans and international education groups support U.S. ratification for these reasons, including the American Veterans (AMVETS), the Air Force Sergeant's Association, the Iraq and Afghanistan Veterans of America, the Vietnam Veterans of America, the Association on Higher Education and Disability, the Disability Law Center, the National Disabilities Rights Network, among others. For a complete list, see *Senate Exec. Rept. 112-6*, pp. 9-12.

[96] Prepared Statement of John L. Wodatch, Former Chief, Disability Rights Section, Civil Rights Division, U.S. Department of Justice, at SFRC hearing, "Convention on the Rights of Persons with Disabilities (Treaty Doc. 112-7)," July 12, 2012.

[97] For more information on the Disabilities Committee, see the "Committee on the Rights of Persons with Disabilities" and "The Role of the Disabilities Committee" sections.

[98] For more information on RUDs, see the "Obama Administration Actions," "Senate Action," and "U.S. Laws Protecting the Rights of Individuals with Disabilities," sections.

[99] *Senate Exec. Rept. 112-6,* pp. 130, 135. For descriptions of these RUDs, see the "Obama Administration Actions" and the "Senate Action" sections.

[100] For example, art. 18 states, "Children with disabilities shall ... have ... the right to know and be cared for by their parents." Art. 23 states, "In no case shall a child be separated from parents on the basis of a disability of either the child or one or both of the parents."

[101] In the minority views of *Senate Exec. Rept. 112-6* (pp. 17-18), for example, some Senators took issue with a 2009 statement by Secretary of State Hillary Clinton before the House Foreign Affairs Committee: "We happen to think that family planning is an important part of women's health, and reproductive health includes access to abortion, that I believe should be safe, legal, and rare."

[102] For more information on existing abortion restrictions in U.S. law, see CRS Report RL33467, *Abortion: Judicial History and Legislative Response*, by Jon O. Shimabukuro, CRS Report 95-724, *Abortion Law Development: A Brief Overview*, by Jon O. Shimabukuro, and CRS Report R41360, *Abortion and Family Planning-Related Provisions in U.S. Foreign Assistance Law and Policy*, by Luisa Blanchfield.

[103] Statement by Ambassador Richard T. Miller, "Explanation of Position on the Convention on the Rights of Persons with Disabilities, Agenda Item 67(b), in the General Assembly," U.S. Mission to the United Nations Press Release #396(06), December 13, 2006.

[104] A list of RUDs by States Parties is available at http://treaties.un.org/Pages/ViewDetails.aspx?src=TREATY& mtdsg_no=IV-15&chapter=4&lang=en#6.105 *Senate Exec. Rept. 112-6,* p. 143.

[106] The proposal was adopted by a SFRC vote of 10 in favor and nine against.

[107] For a description of the debates over the amendments, see *Congressional Quarterly* article by Joanna Anderson, "Senate Panel Supports Ratification of U.N. Treaty on the Disabled, Approves Nominees," July 26, 2012.

[108] See, for example, *Senate Exec. Rept. 112-6,* pp. 17-19 (Minority Views), and Grace Melton, "U.N. Disabilities Treaty Leaves Door Open for Abortion Advocates," *The Heritage Foundation,* August 1, 2012.

[109] Section 2 of Rule XXX states in part that "all proceedings on treaties shall terminate with the Congress, and they shall be resumed at the commencement of the next Congress as if no proceedings had previously been had thereon."

In: The United Nations Convention … ISBN: 978-1-62808-120-6
Editor: Timo Wallner

Chapter 2

TESTIMONY OF JUDITH HEUMANN, SPECIAL ADVISER FOR INTERNATIONAL DISABILITY RIGHTS, U.S. DEPARTMENT OF STATE. HEARING ON "CONVENTION ON THE RIGHTS OF PERSONS WITH DISABILITIES"*

Chairman Kerry, Ranking Member Lugar and Members of the Committee, thank you for the opportunity to appear before you this morning to speak in support of ratification of the Convention on the Rights of Persons with Disabilities, which both the President and the Secretary of State strongly endorse. Ratification of the Disabilities Convention by the United States would be a shining moment in this nation's enduring commitment to advancing and promoting disability rights both at home and abroad. I am privileged to have this opportunity to speak to you on behalf of the Administration, drawing from my life-long personal and professional commitment to promoting the rights of persons with disabilities in the United States and abroad.

As the Special Adviser for International Disability Rights at the U.S. Department of State, I firmly believe ratification will help us to advance our diplomacy abroad, enabling us to highlight how our advances have helped improve the lives of millions of disabled people and their family members. I grew up at a time when our country was just beginning to realize the value of

* This is an edited, reformatted and augmented version of a testimony presented July 12, 2012 before the Senate Foreign Relations Committee.

ensuring the rights of persons with disabilities. Thanks to unstinting leadership from parents and disabled people, and the advocacy of many people, including members of Congress and disabled veterans, we had begun the process of recognizing that our society should respect and promote the dignity, equality and contributions of disabled individuals. However, as a child I did not have the benefit of accessible communities, inclusive schools, or accessible transportation. Without even simple curb cuts, I wheeled in the streets amongst oncoming traffic. I could not ride our buses or trains. I was not allowed to go to school until I was nine years old, and then received poor quality education segregated from the rest of my peers. When I applied for my first job as a teacher, I was initially denied my certification simply because I could not walk.

Today, I am proud to say that such blatant forms of discrimination are no longer permissible in our society. The United States has been a leader in this area.

With strong legislation and effective enforcement honed over more than four decades of experience, Americans with disabilities are respected and included in our society to a degree unrivalled in our history. We can live, work and travel with our fellow citizens, and we see Americans with disabilities serving at the highest levels of government and industry. Unfortunately, the same cannot be said for the majority of the one billion disabled people around the world, or Americans with disabilities, including veterans, who live, work, serve, retire, study, travel, and reside abroad. In developing countries it is estimated that ninety percent of children with disabilities do not attend school. Many disabled children are killed at birth simply because of their disability. I know from my own international work that basic physical access for disabled people is still a dream in many countries, and that enduring cultural stigmas force people with disabilities, who yearn to work and contribute to their families and societies, into abject poverty. I have also experienced first-hand the frustration of travelling in places where it is unfathomable that a significantly disabled person like me would ever leave their home, much less wish to board an international flight.

Against this backdrop of exclusion and discrimination is the vision of progress that we have achieved in the United States, made real through the rule of law, which inspired the international community to draft the Disabilities Convention. At its core, the Convention seeks to ensure that persons with disabilities enjoy the same rights as everyone else and lead their lives as do other individuals, if given the same opportunities. As with the comprehensive network of U.S. federal disability law, the Convention expresses the principles and goals of *inclusion, respect for human dignity and individual autonomy, accessibility, and equal enjoyment of rights*. Equality of opportunity and nondiscrimination are the primary principles permeating both the Convention and U.S. domestic disability law. They animate the important issues addressed by the Convention, including: political participation; access to justice; respect for home and the family; education; access to health care; employment; freedom of expression; and respect for individual autonomy including the freedom to make decisions about how a person wishes to live their life. By requiring equality of opportunity and reasonable accommodation for persons with disabilities, the Convention is reflective of the principles of U.S. disability law, drawn from such core legislation as the Americans with Disabilities Act (ADA), the Rehabilitation Act, and the Individuals with Disabilities Education Act (IDEA). This principle of equality is of course enshrined in the Fifth and Fourteenth Amendments to the United States Constitution.

Given that the Disabilities Convention is animated by the principles underlying U.S. disabilities law, and that it does not create new rights for disabled people, no new legislation would be required to implement the Convention if ratified with the recommended reservations, understandings, and declaration. Significantly, the United States would implement its obligations under existing law; the Convention would not give rise to any new individually enforceable rights. Therefore, you may ask why we should bother to ratify the Convention? Simply put, ratification of the Disabilities Convention will strengthen U.S. interests. It will promote tangible benefits for U.S. business and the approximately 50 million Americans with disabilities, including the 5.5 million American veterans with disabilities, who wish to live, work, serve, retire, study, travel, and reside abroad. By ratifying this Convention we will be putting ourselves in a position to assist our international partners to do as much as we have done domestically to enhance disability rights.

Prior to the adoption of the Convention, fewer than 50 countries around the world had adopted some form of non-discrimination legislation to protect the rights of persons with disabilities. Ratification of the Convention by over 114 countries has since led to a dramatic increase in international interest in addressing the rights of persons with disabilities. However, overall standards of protection around the world typically remain subpar, as does enforcement of the protections that do exist. Such conditions limit opportunities abroad for Americans with disabilities. U.S citizens with disabilities frequently face barriers when they travel, conduct business, study, serve, reside, or retire overseas. With our extensive domestic experience in promoting equality and inclusion of persons with disabilities, the United States is uniquely positioned to help interested countries understand how to effectively comply with their obligations under the Convention. Indeed, provision of such technical assistance and knowledge sharing forms an important part of my work with the Department of State. However, the fact that we have yet to ratify the Disabilities Convention is frequently raised by foreign officials, and deflects from what should be center stage: how their own record of promoting disability rights could be improved. Though I take great pride in the U.S. record, it is frankly difficult to make best use of the "bully pulpit" to challenge disability rights violations on behalf of Americans with disabilities and others, when we have not ratified the Convention. Ratification would give the United States legitimacy and a platform from which to push for the adoption and implementation of the Convention's standards in other countries. This in turn will likely result in concrete improvements (such as fewer architectural barriers and accessible air travel) in those nations that bring their national laws into compliance, thus affording greater protections, opportunities and benefits to the millions of U.S. citizens with disabilities who currently face barriers abroad.

Our failure to ratify has also undermined our advocacy for persons with disabilities in multi-lateral and regional fora, where ratification of the Convention has become a de-facto pre-requisite for meaningful engagement in discussions on promotion of disability rights. For example, by ratifying we would be able to amplify our voice in the Disabilities Convention's Conference of States Parties, to which the United States sends delegations of disability rights experts but currently only as an observer. This severely curtails the role that the United States can play in such meetings, particularly as more countries ratify. By joining the 114 other States Parties to the Convention, we could help shape the international disability agenda by taking a more prominent role in future Conferences, shaping and leading Conference meetings and panel discussions and more actively contributing to the international disability rights dialogue. We will be a leading force in the drive to both improve lives and increase understanding and cooperation among States, as well as to impact the development of international standards on accessibility. Disability diplomacy will have a positive effect on overall bilateral and regional diplomacy of the United States, by allowing us to leverage the shared value of disability rights to promote dialogue on other issues of importance to U.S. foreign policy. We have found that inclusion of disability rights in the work of the State Department amplifies our ability to achieve our broader foreign policy objectives. However, this work is unduly hampered by our not having a seat at the table as a State Party.

Ratification would also be good for American business. By encouraging other countries to join and implement the Convention, we would also help level the playing field to the benefit of U.S. companies. It would enhance the competitive edge for our companies whose operations and hiring already meet accessibility requirements. Guiding and encouraging improved disability standards abroad would also afford U.S. businesses increased opportunities to export innovative products and technologies (such as electronic wheelchairs and other mobility devices, as well as accessible computers and electronics), thereby potentially stimulating job creation at home. As accessibility standards become more harmonized – a business objective that the United States can more credibly support if it becomes a State Party – the competitive edge increases for U.S. companies even further with the opening of markets.

As I travel and meet disabled people from around the world, I am often reminded of how far we have come in the United States over the course of my lifetime, and how far so many countries have yet to go in ensuring that persons with disabilities are full and equal members of their societies. I also meet Americans with disabilities and their family members, who talk of the struggles they have faced abroad to live, work and study with dignity and respect. Just as the ADA and related laws have become the gold standard for domestic disabilities legislation, U.S. ratification of the Disabilities Convention would represent a paradigm shift in the international treatment of persons with disabilities. The treaty is anchored in the overarching principles of inclusion, equality, and nondiscrimination that Americans already value at home. Ratification would serve both to underscore the enduring U.S. commitment to disability rights and to enhance the ability of the United States to promote these rights overseas. U.S. ratification would better position the United States to exercise its leadership role to guide and encourage other countries to ratify and implement the Convention. Leading by example, in what we do and what we say, is a hallmark of America's principles and policies. Any opportunity that we have to positively influence the practice of other countries in respecting the rights of persons with disabilities helps to create a world in which Americans with disabilities can promote American values by pursuing travel, work and study abroad unhindered by the barriers they currently face. Such opportunities can only be enhanced by our ratification of the Disabilities Convention.

In sum, ratification is good for America and good for Americans. It will provide the United States with a critical platform from which to urge other countries to improve equality of individuals with disabilities, including Americans who travel or live abroad, and including children with disabilities, whose plight is particularly neglected in many parts of the world. The transformation which paved the way in the United States for children with disabilities to grow up with their families, go to school, and live as full participants in society has simply not taken place in much of the rest of the world. To promote the rights of individuals with disabilities overseas more effectively, the United States can use its ratification of the Convention as a vehicle to encourage, guide, pressure, and persuade other States Parties to implement better disability standards and provide greater disability rights protection in their countries, including to Americans. Ratification is a win-win, as protections in the United States would not need to be changed, and joining would not affect U.S. sovereignty. Ratification would open up opportunities for U.S. citizens, organizations, and businesses abroad, including our disabled youth, who rightly expect to be full participants in shaping our world's future.

Ratification of the Disabilities Convention would mark a momentous step toward the protection and advancement of the rights of persons with disabilities wherever they may live. It is a significant step for both its profound impact on our diplomatic leadership and for its tangible benefits to everyday Americans. Finally, in keeping with America's long-standing bi-partisan tradition of support for the rights of disabled people, ratification of the Disabilities Convention is the right and just thing to do.

In: The United Nations Convention … ISBN: 978-1-62808-120-6
Editor: Timo Wallner

Chapter 3

STATEMENT OF EVE HILL, SENIOR COUNSELOR TO THE ASSISTANT ATTORNEY GENERAL FOR CIVIL RIGHTS, U.S. DEPARTMENT OF JUSTICE. HEARING ON "CONVENTION ON THE RIGHTS OF PERSONS WITH DISABILITIES"*

Good morning, Chairman Kerry, Ranking Member Lugar, and members of the Committee. Thank you for holding this hearing about the United States' ratification of the U.N. Convention on the Rights of Persons with Disabilities (Disabilities Convention). I am here today to speak to the relationship between the Disabilities Convention and our American disability-rights laws, which served, to a great extent, as the inspiration and model for the Disabilities Convention.

We in the United States are world leaders in the effort to protect the rights of persons with disabilities. Our early initiatives to protect disability rights and the subsequent decades-long effort to enhance disability rights have resulted in a panoply of American laws that protect the rights of persons with disabilities to a greater extent than any other country on the globe. Where many other countries approach disability rights from an aspirational vantage, we match our legislation with concrete, effective enforcement mechanisms that have led to visible, notable changes in our society in our lifetimes. Curb cuts, ramps,

* This is an edited, reformatted and augmented version of a statement presented July 12, 2012 before the Senate Foreign Relations Committee.

accessible parking spaces, American Sign Language interpreters, service animals – these are just a few of the ground-breaking changes that have swept through our society thanks to our vigorous enforcement of disability-rights laws.

While we in the United States too often take the tremendous advances in disability rights for granted, much work remains to be done and the Department of Justice and other Federal agencies are actively addressing discrimination on the basis of disability arising in a variety of arenas. These implementation efforts are driven by domestic law and practice and this approach would not change with the ratification of the Disabilities Convention. The Americans with Disabilities Act (ADA) addresses the disability nondiscrimination obligations of State and local governmental entities, including educational institutions, local government offices, parks, libraries, hospitals, nursing homes, and more, and by private entities, including stores, restaurants, recreational facilities, banks, and other providers of goods and services. The ADA also prohibits disability discrimination by employers with 15 or more employees. Our disability-rights laws affect more than six million businesses and nonprofit agencies, 80,000 units of State and local government, and 54 million people with disabilities. In addition, our Federal government has been committed to disability rights in its own programs and services, as well as those it funds, for decades through the Rehabilitation Act of 1973, the Architectural Barriers Act, and many other Federal laws.

Along with the Department of Justice, a panoply of other Federal agencies and entities are engaged in efforts to address discrimination on the basis of disability, including the Department of Housing and Urban Development, the Department of Education the Department of Veterans Affairs, the Department of Health and Human Services, the Department of Transportation, the Federal Communications Commission, the U.S. Access Board, and the Equal Employment Opportunity Commission (EEOC), each of which takes on significant responsibilities for the enforcement of our domestic disability-rights laws.

The Disabilities Convention is firmly grounded in, and animated by, the principles underlying U.S. disabilities laws, including the Rehabilitation Act of 1973, the ADA, and the Individuals with Disabilities Education Act. Therefore, ratifying the Disabilities Convention will not require new legislation and will not create any new rights, so long as it moves forward with the recommended Reservations, Understandings, and Declaration (or RUDs). The Convention was finalized in December 2006 after several years of drafting and negotiations, during which a U.S. delegation played an active role and joined in the consensus adoption of the Convention. The influence of U.S. disability law on the Disabilities Convention is apparent in the way the Convention mirrors our robust and well-developed U.S. disability-rights legislation. The Disabilities Convention follows the core principles of U.S. disability-rights laws – equality of treatment and nondiscrimination, with an emphasis throughout the Convention of rights provided "on an equal basis with others." It incorporates concepts central to U.S. disability-rights law, such as independent living, inclusive education, and reasonable accommodation, limited, as it is in U.S. law, by the qualification that an accommodation need not be made if it entails undue burden or expense.

The Administration has proposed that the Senate consider a package of three Reservations, five Understandings, and one Declaration that will allow the United States to be in full compliance with the Convention without any changes to U.S. law. These are detailed in the transmittal package, but I would like to speak to three of them today.

First, the package includes a federalism reservation, similar to the federalism RUDs that were taken with the ratification of the International Covenant on Civil and Political Rights (ICCPR) and the Convention on the Elimination of All Forms of Racial Discrimination (CERD). This federalism reservation would limit the obligations of the United States in areas covered by State and local government jurisdiction to measures appropriate to the Federal system, maintaining the current allocation of authority between the Federal Government and the 50 States. While we have a significant network of Federal disability laws, some treaty articles would be primarily implemented under State laws, such as Article 12, which addresses guardianship, and Article 14, which addresses civil commitment. In most cases, State and local laws and practices meet or exceed the requirements of Federal law and thus the Convention. In instances governed primarily by state law where some State and local protections may be less robust than the Convention would require, such as regarding Article 12(4), which addresses safeguards in determinations of legal capacity, the federalism reservation would preserve the existing balance of authority between the Federal Government and the States. As we have observed, led by the advances at the Federal level, the dominant trend in State and local disability-rights laws has been toward improvement and modernization. Thus, while the adoption of a federalism reservation will allow us to adopt the Disabilities Convention without any new legislation, it in no way will impede us from continuing forward progress in disability rights protection.

I would also like to underscore the recommended reservation on private conduct. Similar to a reservation taken in treaties already ratified, such as the ICCPR and CERD, the private-conduct reservation is intended to ensure that regulation of the conduct of private parties under the Convention, including businesses and nongovernmental organizations, is co-extensive with such regulation under existing domestic law. United States law extensively governs significant areas of nongovernmental activity, such as disability discrimination by public accommodations, transport carriers, communications networks, and employers. At the same time, the U.S. Constitution and laws recognize a zone of private activity that is not extensively governed by Federal or State government, and, in some cases, expressly enjoys constitutional protection. This important reservation, therefore, would limit the treaty obligations undertaken by the United States respecting regulation of private conduct to be coextensive with such regulation under the Constitution and domestic laws of the United States. As the EEOC has separately confirmed to the Committee, with the proposed RUD package, the United States will rely on existing law to fully comply with the Disabilities Convention. (See the attached letter from the EEOC.)

Third, I also would like to address the proposed non-self-executing Declaration which would make it clear that the Convention could not be directly enforced by U.S. courts and would not give rise to individually enforceable rights. This is consistent with our treaty practice under the ICCPR, CERD, and the Convention Against Torture. With this Declaration and the other Reservations and Understandings, the United States would be able to implement its obligations under the Disabilities Convention using the existing network of laws and Federal enforcement machinery that afford protection and guarantees of nondiscrimination to persons with disabilities. As such, no new legislation would be required to ratify and implement the Convention.

With the ratification of the Disabilities Convention, we will greatly enhance our capacity to influence other countries to move towards the vigorous, effective standards we have set at home. In turn, as other countries move forward, American veterans, business people, retirees, students, tourists, active-duty military, and others will be able to enjoy the same kinds of accessibility and nondiscrimination overseas that they currently enjoy in the United States. Thus, with the ratification of the Disabilities Convention, we will level the playing field for American businesses that are already complying with accessibility standards and provide new opportunities for the export of accessible technology.

Protection of the rights of persons with disabilities has historically been grounded in bipartisan support and the principles anchoring the Convention find clear expression in our own domestic law. We therefore urge that this Committee give prompt and favorable consideration to this Convention, and that the full Senate give its advice and consent to its ratification, subject to the Administration's proposed reservations, understandings, and declaration.

In: The United Nations Convention … ISBN: 978-1-62808-120-6
Editor: Timo Wallner

Chapter 4

TESTIMONY OF DICK THORNBURGH, FORMER ATTORNEY GENERAL OF THE UNITED STATES. HEARING ON "CONVENTION ON THE RIGHTS OF PERSONS WITH DISABILITIES"*

It is a distinct pleasure for to me to testify in favor of the ratification of the Convention on the Rights of Persons with Disabilities (the Convention or CRPD) as an important component of the worldwide effort to advance disability rights.

Ratification by this body would mark a major step forward in the effort to end discrimination and to promote the rights of as many as one billion men, women and children with disabilities around the world who seek vindication of their pre-eminent human rights in an ever-challenging world.

To date, as I last looked, a total of 153 countries (including the United States) have signed the Convention and 116 have ratified its terms. We literally stand today at the very cusp of a new era of worldwide recognition of disability rights.

A major leap forward in this effort would be accomplished by timely U.S. Senate ratification of the Convention.

---

* This is an edited, reformatted and augmented version of a testimony presented July 12, 2012 before the Senate Foreign Relations Committee.

I.

The road to this point has been a lengthy one and I think it may be useful to review how we have gotten to where we are as a means of aiding the process of further progress. In another context, a great American jurist, Supreme Court Justice Oliver Wendell Holmes, Jr. once observed, “A page of history is worth a volume of logic,” and in this movement as well I suggest that some history is an appropriate starting point.

As many of you may know, I have been involved in the disability movement for many years. I was a founding director of the National Organization on Disability back in 1982 and later served as Vice Chairman of its international arm, the World Committee on Disability. I am also the father of a man with intellectual and physical disability – my son, Peter who was seriously brain-injured at the age of four months in a 1960 automobile accident which tragically took the life of his mother, my first wife.

As Governor of Pennsylvania and Attorney General of the United States, I have had the privilege to work in official capacities for the inclusion of people with disabilities in all aspects of life. Indeed, it was my special privilege to serve as the point person for the administration of President George H. W. Bush in the bi-partisan effort to secure the passage of the Americans with Disabilities Act (ADA) in 1990. This work has become a bit of a family affair, as my present wife, Ginny, whom I married in 1963, founded the Religion and Disability Program of the National Organization on Disability, designed to insure spiritual and religious access to persons with physical, mental and intellectual disability. She is now the Director of the Interfaith Initiative at the American Association of People with Disabilities coordinating efforts by leaders of all faiths to advance the cause of disability rights. In her responsibility as Convener of the Interfaith Disability Advocacy Coalition (IDAC), she enlisted 26 religious or religiously-affiliated organizations to send a letter of support for the Convention to members of this Committee. We have thus had the great privilege of merging our personal and career objectives in this worthy cause.

It is obvious that the world community has taken an important – and long overdue –step toward bringing people with disabilities all over the world into the mainstream of the human rights movement by adopting this Convention. I must applaud the disability community for its tireless efforts in what must have seemed at times to be an uphill battle for international recognition of this important principle.

I know first hand from my service as an Under-Secretary General at the United Nations in the immediate post-Cold War era of the long struggle to obtain passage of this Convention. The effort had its genesis in the 1981 Year of Disabled Persons, followed by the Decade of Disabled Persons and the promulgation of the World Programme of Action Concerning Disabled Persons, all providing focal points for efforts to internationalize concerns about disability rights. I particularly recall attending the historic gathering in Montreal in October of 1992 of the very first International Conference of Ministers Responsible for the Status of Persons With Disabilities where 73 leaders of governments throughout the world met for the first time to exchange ideas and fashion strategies which ultimately led to the adoption of the Convention.

The Convention represents important principles that as Americans we hold dear – basic recognition and equal protection of every person under the law, non-discrimination, the fundamental importance of independent living, and the right to make basic choices about our lives. We pioneered these basic principles under American law through passage of the ADA. We in the United States are demonstrating that people with disabilities can participate fully in our democracy. We are demonstrating that society, as a whole, is richer and better off when people with disabilities are included fully in every aspect of life. It is my hope and expectation that the United States will assume an equally important leadership role in helping to promote these basic principles worldwide by the ratification of this Convention.

Over 20 years ago, while serving as U.S. Attorney General, I testified before House and Senate Committees of the U.S. Congress in support of the ADA. During those hearings I acknowledged that no piece of legislation could alone change the long-standing misperceptions that many people have about disability – misperceptions based largely on stereotype, ignorance and fear of what is different. Any reshaping of attitudes would have to be the gradual result not of the words or ideas in the laws, but of bringing people with disabilities from the margins of society into the mainstream of American life – in our schools and workplaces, on busses and trains, and in our courthouses, restaurants, theaters and congregations – where they not only have an absolute right to be but where we have an obligation as fellow human beings to welcome them as equals.

The effort to secure passage of the ADA was difficult. Those of us who wanted to see it happen were given countless reasons why it couldn't be done. We were told that the climate in Congress wasn't right, it would be too expensive, too complicated, ineffective, impossible to enforce – even that the country in general just wasn't ready for it. So we discussed, debated, argued, researched, analyzed, negotiated, pleaded, convinced and, ultimately, drafted and passed the most progressive disability rights legislation the world had ever seen. This legislation, with its innovative concepts such as the need for "reasonable accommodation," is changing America. It has truly made us more representative, more democratic and more empowering by ending the unchecked exclusion of 54 million Americans from our daily lives.

Of course we still have a long way to go in our own country. The ADA isn't perfect and people with disabilities in America continue to face serious challenges. Court decisions have sometimes hindered the full implementation of the ADA and required legislative responses such as the 2008 ADA Amendments Act. Still, in the years following 1990, we've made remarkable progress that is not only celebrated here at home but also recognized abroad. Because of our adoption of the ADA and other disability rights legislation, the United States is viewed internationally as a pioneering role model for disability rights. Disability activists from other countries have taken the ADA to their governments and said, "This is how it should be done. We need to do this here in our country." And governments around the world have responded. As one who worked hard to gain protection of these rights in the United States, I am very proud to see how these basic principles are now on the way to being established as a part of international law through the adoption of the CRPD. As we overcame so many barriers to the enactment and implementation of the ADA, I am confident that we can be part of an even greater coalition to bring about worldwide support for this Convention as well.

Despite progress already made, disability as a global issue remains near the bottom of the list of priorities in many governments and societies. People with disabilities remain among the poorest, least educated and most abused and excluded people on earth. We must recognize that the challenges we face are intimately linked with the very circumstances of economic, social, and political marginalization that affect people with disabilities around the world.

While the adoption of the CPRD represents a truly significant accomplishment for the international community and a great source of hope for people with disabilities everywhere, it will obviously not be enough. Between the adoption of the convention and the actual securing of the important rights its seeks to guarantee will no doubt lie a long and tortuous path which will test the commitment, tenacity and political will of the international community – from national leaders to grass roots advocacy organizations to individual citizens bent upon justice for all.

However, we must also keep in mind that the Convention can be a strong tool – as well as an inspiration – for civil society around the world. NGOs and advocates will have a new legal framework within which to push for reforms based on legal obligations.

II.

Let me address for a moment the painful and, I must admit, somewhat puzzling question of the seeming reluctance of some in our own nation to continue our lead role in this international effort. Let's look at some of the questions and concerns that have been raised about this convention as it has reached this body for ratification.

To begin with, it has been argued that disability rights are more appropriately addressed a solely a domestic concern, given the complexity of the issues involved. In other words, this really isn't an appropriate subject for international protection. Certainly, good domestic legislation in every country would be the ideal solution. But since many countries don't have such protections, it does not seem reasonable to expect that this will change dramatically without international pressure. The fact is, for many countries, international conventions have already served as a catalyst for the development of important domestic protections in many other areas.

As a practical matter, the United States will have much more authority to speak out about these and other forms of discrimination against people with disabilities worldwide if we agree to abide by the same international scrutiny at home. We already have laws in place that are consistent with the CRPD. But, it is correctly noted that by ratifying the Convention, the United States agrees to report regularly to an international advisory body. We have nothing to hide. We can only gain from participating in the process of international review. Moreover, we should not be so proud as to think that we cannot learn from other countries about how to meet the challenge of providing even better opportunities for people with disabilities.

Some have looked at the final text of the convention and found it lacking in strict, enforceable protections. Some say that it lacks the kind of detail that we fought so hard to include in the ADA and that we have found so essential for the enforcement of basic rights in the United States. We must keep in mind that a human rights convention is a legal instrument that must apply consistently around the world – in countries rich and poor, in countries with widely varying legal systems, in many countries where the idea of full participation for people with disabilities may be radically new and untested. The flexibility of this convention is its strength – not its weakness. It lays down the core values and principles that are essential to ending discrimination against people with disabilities in any society. It provides governments with guidance and direction now lacking under the general provisions of international law. Article 9, for example, requires governments to "take appropriate measures to ensure to persons with disabilities access, on an equal basis with others, to the physical environment, to transportation, to information and communications ... and to other facilities and services open or provided to the public, both in urban and in rural areas." Article 24 recognizes the rights of persons with disabilities to education and requires governments to provide "an inclusive education system at all levels ... [e]nabling persons with disabilities to participate effectively in a free society."

The Convention provides governments with core, minimum standards needed to make essential reforms without locking different countries into one particular approach or another. As noted, the Convention creates a Committee on the Rights of Persons with Disabilities that will review reports of governments and will issue general recommendations about how to bring about full compliance with the Convention. Through this process of interpretation, governments at every level of economic and social development can receive guidance about steps they can take to bring about enforcement of the Convention.

At the same time, it is important to note that ratification of the Convention will require no new domestic legislation and will impose no new costs upon U.S. taxpayers. As does our own ADA, the Convention simply ensures non-discrimination on the basis of disability, guaranteeing that persons with disabilities enjoy the same rights as other persons.

Finally, some have said that, because of America's comprehensive domestic protections, a treaty on disability would have no relevance in our own country. But, let's hold on a minute. We are indeed at this time the most progressive country in the world when it comes to the domestic protection of disability rights. The universality of rights and fundamental freedoms – as expressed in our Declaration of Independence – is the foundation on which our entire society is based. Respect for human rights is also a stated principle of our foreign policy – pbecause we recognize that stability, security and economic opportunity in any society presuppose a social order based on respect for the rights of its citizens. Given this history and these values, it would seem natural for the United States to assume a *leading* role – not a passive one - in the effort to recognize and enforce an international treaty of this kind.

Misgivings expressed by critics of the Convention have already been addressed in reservations, understandings and declarations (RUDs) contained in the package submitted by the administration. By addressing federalism, providing a zone of private action protected by the Constitution and declaring the Convention to be non-self executing, these RUDs protect U.S. sovereignty and recognize the Convention as a non-discrimination instrument, similar to our own ADA.

Ratification of the Disability Rights Convention is an opportunity to export to the world the very best we have to offer. This is a chance to use our rich national experience in disability rights – which has gained us the respect of the world community - to extend the principles embodied in the ADA to the hundreds of millions of people with disabilities worldwide who today have no domestic protection. This is worthy of our leadership. We have everything to gain and nothing to lose by playing the role the world expects of us. We must ratify the Convention so that we can fulfill that role.

III.

Just as in the case of the ADA, we must recognize that the Convention will not provide instant legal solutions which can effect immediate changes in attitudes and cultural perceptions; nor will it dispel the ignorance that leads to discrimination and human rights abuses of people with disabilities. What it will do is create a permanent place for disability within the human rights framework. It will put disability issues on the radar screen of governments and societies recisely as a legitimate human rights concern to which they must pay heed. It will provide guidance and standards and create legal obligations for governments to respect the rights of this sizable population. It can serve as a powerful advocacy tool for the global disability movement to promote inclusion and equality of opportunity.

Before closing let me say a word, in particular, about the developing nations of the world wherein, it is estimated, some 80% of the world's disabled population lives. Most of these persons are at the margin of their respective societies. Priority concerns of just surviving – combating hunger, securing shelter and eking out a daily existence – unfortunately take present precedence over concerns for people with disabilities.

It is sometimes said that, in nations struggling with a full agenda of political and economic problems and the effort to achieve basic human rights for all their citizens, the interests of persons with disabilities are likely to be set to one side for "future consideration," *i.e.*, when these other more important matters have been addressed.

On the contrary, I would suggest that what responsible leaders of developing nations need to realize is the unique opportunity they have to embed disability rights in their emerging institutions as part of their development efforts, to build an infrastructure of government, economy and human rights that includes and respects the interests of persons with disabilities from the very beginning. For it is no exaggeration to say that the way a society treats its citizens with disabilities is a valid measure of the quality of life and respect for human dignity in that society.

Even after ratification and implementation of the Convention, change will be gradual – and perhaps painfully slow, to be sure, but these represent important first steps we can take toward promoting change on a global scale. This Convention can help all of us to focus world attention on those millions of people worldwide whose rights have been ignored for far too long. Let's be about the business of seeing that those rights are honored, and implemented, now and forever more, by providing timely ratification of this important Convention.

Thank you for your attention.

In: The United Nations Convention …
Editor: Timo Wallner
ISBN: 978-1-62808-120-6

Chapter 5

TESTIMONY OF JOHN L. WODATCH, FORMER CHIEF OF THE DISABILITY RIGHTS SECTION, CIVIL RIGHTS DIVISION, U.S. DEPARTMENT OF JUSTICE. HEARING ON "CONVENTION ON THE RIGHTS OF PERSONS WITH DISABILITIES"*

Mr. Chairman and Members of the Committee:

Thank you for your invitation to present my views to the Committee. I come before you this morning to urge you to support ratification of the Convention on the Rights of Persons with Disabilities.

I have a long history of work on disability rights issues. I have witnessed firsthand the strong bipartisan support for disability rights that is out nation's tradition. I retired last July from service in the federal executive branch after 42 years of service. During that time I was the author of the federal government's first comprehensive disability rights regulations, regulations implementing Section 504 of the Rehabilitation Act, first issued in 1977. I was fortunate to work for Attorney General Dick Thornburgh during our nation's consideration of the Americans with Disabilities Act and served as a member of the White House team under President George H.W. Bush that negotiated the ADA. I then oversaw development of the ADA regulations and served as

* This is an edited, reformatted and augmented version of testimony given on July 12, 2012 before the Senate Foreign Relations Committee.

the head of the new unit at the Department of Justice that was created to implement the ADA. I also served as a member of the U.S. delegation that negotiated the Convention on the Rights of Persons with Disabilities.

I. The Disabilities Convention and U.S. Disability Rights Law

The Disabilities Convention is modeled on the disability rights laws of the United States and adopts the successful and balanced approach of U.S. federal disability rights law dating back to 1977. It embodies the traditional American ideals that form the basis of the Americans with Disabilities Act and other U.S. disability rights laws. These include the core principles of nondiscrimination and equality of opportunity. The treaty seeks to empower persons with disabilities to be independent, to claim personal responsibility for their own lives, and to be able to make their own choices.

The Americans with Disabilities Act, or ADA, is a comprehensive civil rights law protecting the rights of persons with disabilities in the United States. Since it was signed into law in 1990 by President George H. W. Bush, it has literally changed the landscape of this country, opening up everyday American life to persons with disabilities.

The ADA is, however, just one part of a rich and varied series of federal protections of the rights of person with disabilities. The Architectural Barriers Act of 1968 ensures that Federal buildings will be accessible according to strict Federal design standards. The Individuals with Disabilities Education Act ensures that children with disabilities will receive a free, appropriate education. The Fair Housing Act ensures that people with disabilities will have accessible housing. The Air Carrier Access Act opens air travel to persons with disabilities. The Help America Vote Act, as well as the Voting Accessibility for the Elderly and Handicapped Act of 1984, provide for an accessible electoral process, including accessible polling places. The ADA and title V of the Rehabilitation Act provide a comprehensive framework, covering employment, transportation, public accommodations, telephone service, and all the activities of State and local governments to persons with disabilities.

These laws have proven to be a success because they are grounded in nondiscrimination principles, and they provide a balanced approach to accessibility. Each requirement is tempered by limitations that reflect the difficulty and costs of achieving accessibility. Thus the obligation to make reasonable accommodation to employees is limited by undue hardship. Businesses do not have to make changes to their programs and services if they are too costly or would fundamentally change the nature of the program or service. Small employers (under 15 employees) are exempted from all requirements as are churches, other religious entities, and purely private clubs.

I was fortunate to be a member of the U.S. delegation to the UN Ad Hoc Committee that was considering the formulation of a disabilities convention. The Committee deliberated from 2001 to 2006, when the treaty was adopted by the UN. The Bush Administration charged us with two main tasks -- to provide assistance in the development of the new treaty and to ensure that the treaty reflect the core concepts of American disability law. We successfully followed President Bush's directions: the Disabilities Convention follows our U.S. principles. Its focus is nondiscrimination, ensuring that persons with disabilities enjoy the same rights as other citizens. Like the ADA, its rights are tempered by limitations. Reasonable accommodation is required but only if the modification is necessary and appropriate and only if it does not impose a disproportionate or undue burden. While the treaty does not itself contain a definition of disability, its guidelines for what constitutes a person with a disability conform closely to the definitions found in U.S law. In fact, the revised ADA definition of a person with a disability, adopted in 2008 in the Americans with Disabilities Act Amendments Act, and signed into law by President Bush, fully comply with the concepts of the treaty.

And the comprehensive nature of the treaty mirrors the U.S. approach to disability rights. Both recognize that persons with disabilities will not be able to enjoy equal opportunity unless there is broad coverage. Having an education loses its meaning if jobs are foreclosed to students with disabilities. Nondiscrimination in employment will not be meaningful unless persons can get to work on accessible transportation. Having a job will lose its meaning if persons are unable to enjoy the fruits of their labor, from dining at a restaurant, going to a movie, or traveling across the country. Thus, then, like U.S. law, the Disabilities Convention is comprehensive in its approach. It addresses access to facilities, political participation, access to justice, access to education, employment, health care, participation in public and cultural life, recreation, leisure activities, and sports. It upholds freedom of expression, access to information, the ability to live independently in one's own community, and freedom from torture and other cruel, inhuman, or degrading treatment.

In sum, the Disabilities Convention is an embodiment of the nondiscrimination principles developed in the United States. Its principles and, indeed, its language, come directly from U.S. law.

II. Reservations, Understandings, and Declarations

The Administration's submission of the Disabilities Convention, which includes the President's letter of transmittal and the Secretary of State's Report, makes clear that the convention is exclusively a nondiscrimination treaty, i.e., the Disabilities Convention seeks to ensure that persons with disabilities enjoy the same rights as everyone else and are given the same opportunities to live productive lives. The Secretary's Report includes reservations, understandings, and a declaration (RUDs) recommended for inclusion in the Senate's resolution of advice and consent. Inclusion of these RUDs will facilitate ratification. Under the RUDs, U.S. obligations under the Convention will go no further than existing U.S. law.

The package of three reservations, five understandings, and one declaration, contained in the Secretary's Report, maintains U.S. sovereignty and makes clear the extent of our obligations under the treaty and are thus an essential element of ratification. With the inclusion of this RUD package:

> No new federal laws will be required to comply with the treaty; No State laws will have to be revised;
>
> Compliance with our existing, rich panoply of disability laws will constitute compliance with the treaty;
>
> Our definitions of disability will continue in force; and
>
> No new individual rights and no individually enforceable rights will be created.

These RUDs also ensure that ratification will have no impact on the federal budget. Thus, I recommend that the Senate Resolution of Advice and Consent to Ratification contain the nine RUDs proposed in the Secretary's Report.

Perhaps the two most important reservations are those recommended on federalism and on private conduct. A number of treaty provisions cover matters that are the province of State law. For example, education, the exercise of legal capacity, civil commitment, birth registration, living in the community, and marriage and family relationships are areas that are governed in the United States under State law. While many state and local laws and regulations clearly comply with the provisions of the Disabilities Convention on these issues, some state and local standards can be interpreted as less rigorous than the treaty would require. Thus, a reservation that would preserve the existing balance between federal and state jurisdiction over these matters is appropriate and necessary.

The federalism reservation ensures that the obligations undertaken by the United States upon ratification would be implemented in a manner consistent with the existing allocation of authority between the federal government and the fifty states. The federalism reservation would limit our obligations under the treaty to areas covered by federal law and would require no changes to state and local law because of the Convention's provisions.

The proposed reservation on certain private conduct is also important. A number of federal disability rights laws contain exemptions in their coverage. Title I of the ADA applies to all employers with 15 or more employees. Title III of the ADA does not apply to churches and other religious entities and certain private clubs. The Fair Housing Act does not apply to most individuals' homes or private home construction. Similarly, the U.S. Constitution and federal law recognize areas of private activity that are not governed by the laws of the United States. It is thus necessary and appropriate to include a reservation that limits coverage of the treaty and excludes those areas of private conduct that are protected by the U.S. Constitution.

Similarly significant is the declaration that the Convention on the Rights of Persons with Disabilities is non-self-executing. This declaration ensures that the treaty itself does not give rise to individually enforceable rights and cannot be directly enforced in the U.S. courts. It ensures the primacy of U.S. domestic law and remedies on disability issues.

In the last several weeks, the treaty has been criticized for undermining U.S. sovereignty and for harming the rights of parents of children with disabilities. These concerns can be fully addressed by the terms of the treaty, by the RUDs proposed by the Administration, and by the clarifications contained in the Secretary's report.

Some have raised alarms over the existence of the Disabilities Committee created by the treaty. This committee, a group of 18 experts elected by the nation's that have ratified the treaty, meets twice each year to review the reports submitted by those countries that have ratified the treaty. By the terms of the treaty itself this committee is advisory only. The committee is authorized only to respond to reports with "suggestions and general recommendations." The Committee's suggestions, observations, and opinions are not binding and cannot compel any action in the United States.

The criticism that the treaty will undermine parental decision-making is misplaced. In fact, the treaty places great value on the role of the family. The Preamble to the treaty is particularly eloquent on this issue. It states:

> (T)he family is the natural and fundamental group unit of society and is entitled to protection by society and the State, and that persons with disabilities and their family members should receive the necessary protection and assistance to enable families to contribute toward the full and equal enjoyment of the rights of persons with disabilities.

The treaty specifically requires ratifying nations to provide early and comprehensive information, services, and support to children with disabilities and their families. It seeks to maintain the sanctity of the family unit by requiring that children should not be separated from their parents on the basis of the disability of either the parents or the children.

Most importantly, the overarching requirement of Article 23 of the treaty is one of nondiscrimination. The Convention, like Title II of the ADA, prohibits discrimination against persons with disabilities in matters of family and parenthood. Further, the proposed reservation on federalism ensures that parental responsibility and authority, which are matters of state and local law, will remain governed by domestic law in the United States. Also, the reservation on private conduct ensures that privacy in family matters, which is protected by the U.S. Constitution, will not be encumbered by the treaty. The Secretary's Report specifically addresses family rights in its discussion of Article 23 (at p. 53) and notes that freedom from governmental interference in certain private conduct is among the fundamental values of our free and democratic society.

One other concern that has been raised warns of a threat of a national registry of children with disabilities. The treaty does not require a national registry of births in the U.S. Birth registration is handled by the states, which are subject to the disability nondiscrimination requirements of Title II of the ADA and Section 504 of the Rehabilitation Act. State laws on birth registration require that each child be given a birth certificate at birth - thus they are recognized as a person, protected by law. The treaty does not require a separate registration of children with disabilities, something the United States has consistently refused to support. Therefore, the treaty will not result in any change in U.S. or state law or practice. However, the treaty will provide much-needed protection in other countries where there is no provision for birth certificates or birth registration for children with disabilities. In particular, it will help protect against the horrible practice of infanticide of children born with disabilities (a practice that can be facilitated through the denial of birth certificates or registration to disabled babies), and it will require equal access to immunizations, education, food, and other essential needs for these children.

These reservations are eminently reasonable and are compatible with the object and purpose of the treaty. And once included in the Senate Resolution of Advice and Consent, these reservations become the law. While other ratifying nations may seek to object to a reservation, no nation nor any international body has the ability or power to sever, amend, or overturn such a reservation.

One other issue that has raised concerns about the Disabilities Convention is how it may apply to the issue of family planning and abortion. The treaty affirms the inherent right to life and recognizes the "dignity and worth" of persons with disabilities. It establishes for the first time internationally that ratifying nations cannot discriminatorily deny health care, health services, or food and fluids on the basis of disability. During the debate at the Ad Hoc Committee of the UN, the Treaty Chairman, Ambassador Don McKay of New Zealand, stated that the treaty does not create a right to abortion. The Secretary's Report confirms this interpretation at p. 61 and makes clear that Article 25 does not address the matter of abortion and does not affect United States law with regard to abortion.

III. Benefits of Ratification

So why ratify? I strongly believe that ratification of the Disabilities Convention is in the best interests of the United States, provides protections for Americans with disabilities, and promotes U.S. business interests.

Our failure to ratify the Disabilities Convention, which so clearly follows the pattern of disability rights laws and programs pioneered in the United States, has hampered the position of the United States as a world leader on disability rights issues. While the ADA will continue to be the linchpin of US domestic nondiscrimination policy, the international community uses the treaty as the basis for legal and policy approaches to disability policy. Ratification will enable the United States to have an official place at the table and share our experience with other ratifying nations as they shape emerging disability rights policies and laws in their countries. It will enable us to seek a place on the Disabilities Committee (which is only open to experts from countries that have ratified) and focus the efforts of the Committee on fundamental and important issues.

Ratification will also allow the United States to take a more proactive role in the protection of U.S citizens abroad. Persons with disabilities, including our veterans, now work, study, travel, serve, and retire across the world. But our citizens still face limited opportunities and architectural barriers. An active U.S presence on implementation of the Disabilities Convention will help ensure that our citizens and service members will encounter fewer architectural barriers and a more welcoming environment.

Ratification of the treaty will also help U.S. businesses take advantage of the potential benefits of the treaty. Estimates of the number of persons with disabilities across the world now reach one billion persons. As these persons receive opportunities in their countries, they will need accessible devices, from wheelchairs and other mobility aids and services to new technologies, including smart phones and accessible software for their computers. Many of these products are engineered, made, or sold by U.S. corporations, who will benefit from an active U.S. presence to reach this emerging new source of revenue.

Ratification and the concomitant reemergence of U.S. leadership will also help American multinational corporations level the playing field. For the past twenty-two years American companies have followed a number of domestic requirements, including reasonable accommodation for their workers and accessible facilities for their customers. Unfortunately, their foreign counterparts did not have to follow such a regimen. Ratification of the Convention will enable the U.S. more actively to ensure that other nations that have ratified the Convention actually take the steps to enforce the treaty's accessibility and employment provisions and provide a level playing field for American companies.

Additionally, ratification and an active American presence can result in economies of scale for U.S. companies. Many U.S. multinational companies, including quick service restaurants and hotel chains, create and implement standard design plans for their U.S. facilities, but face different requirements for their building in other countries.

Ratification will enable the United States to push for consistent accessible standards for buildings and create the ability for U.S. multinational companies to follow one template for their accessibility requirements worldwide, resulting in cost savings.

Ratification of the Convention presents an opportunity for the Senate and the President to reaffirm the traditional American values of the treaty, nondiscrimination and equality of opportunity, and provides a forum to advance these values worldwide. The package of RUDs sent forward by the Administration and the specific interpretations found in the Secretary's Report address the concerns that have been identified by outside observers regarding safeguarding American sovereignty and U.S. law.

The Disabilities Convention has been ratified by 115 nations. The time for Senate action to ratify this treaty is now. When he signed the ADA on July 26, 1990, President George H.W. Bush said: "Let the shameful wall of exclusion finally come tumbling down." The words and concepts that he signed into law are now in the laws and constitutions of countries around the world and form the basis for the Disabilities Convention. It is time for the United States to reposition itself as a world leader to help bring down these walls of exclusion for all nations around the globe and help make the world accessible for Americans with disabilities, including our veterans, and for American multinational businesses.

Thank you for your attention.

In: The United Nations Convention … ISBN: 978-1-62808-120-6
Editor: Timo Wallner

Chapter 6

STATEMENT OF STEVEN GROVES, BERNARD AND BARBARA LOMAS FELLOW, THE HERITAGE FOUNDATION. HEARING ON "CONVENTION ON THE RIGHTS OF PERSONS WITH DISABILITIES"*

Mr. Chairman and members of the Committee:

Thank you for inviting me to testify before you today regarding the Convention on the Rights of Persons with Disabilities (CRPD or Convention).

I had the opportunity to testify before this Committee a month ago regarding U.S. accession to the United Nations Convention on the Law of the Sea. While there are no similarities between the two conventions in terms of scope or subject matter, the central question regarding the propriety of U.S. ratification remains the same—whether membership in the convention protects, preserves, or advances U.S. national interests.

The United States should not ratify the CRPD if membership would not advance U.S. national interests at home or abroad. The Administration concedes that U.S. membership in the Convention would not advance the cause of persons with disabilities living in the United States since the United States already has in place comprehensive statutory, regulatory, and enforcement mechanisms regarding disability rights.

* This is an edited, reformatted and augmented version of a statement presented July 12, 2012 before the Senate Foreign Relations Committee.

The question remains whether membership in the Convention would advance national interests in the international sphere. Joining the Convention is unlikely to advance U.S. national interests abroad, but instead would obligate the United States to answer to a committee of "disability experts" in violation of principles of U.S. sovereignty. The United States need not become party to the Convention to demonstrate its strong commitment to disability rights to the international community. Nor is there any evidence that U.S. ratification would enhance the ability of the U.S. government or non-governmental organizations to promote disability rights in foreign countries.

The Convention

On December 13, 2006, the United Nations General Assembly adopted the CRPD "to promote, protect and ensure the full and equal enjoyment of all human rights and fundamental freedoms by all persons with disabilities, and to promote respect for their inherent dignity."[1]

The terms of the Convention are meant to protect the rights of persons with disabilities in the civil, political, economic, social and cultural spheres. It recognizes traditional civil and political rights that are guaranteed under the U.S. Constitution—such as the right to life and liberty, equality before the law, and the freedom of expression and opinion[2]—alongside certain economic, social, and cultural "positive rights," such as the right to education, health, and "an adequate standard of living for [persons with disabilities] and their families, including adequate food, clothing and housing, and to the continuous improvement of living conditions."[3]

The Convention entered into force on May 3, 2008, after 20 nations had deposited their instruments of ratification. The Convention currently has 117 parties, and an additional 36 nations, including the United States, have signed but not ratified the treaty.[4] U.S. Ambassador to the United Nations Susan Rice signed the Convention on July 30, 2009.[5] President Obama transmitted the Convention, an article-by-article analysis, and a set of recommended reservations, declarations, and understandings to the Senate for its advice and consent on or about May 17, 2012 (Transmittal Package).[6]

If the Senate gives its advice and consent and the Convention is ratified, it would become the "supreme Law of the Land" on par with federal statutes, including statutes relating to disability rights.[7] When the United States becomes party to a human rights treaty it obligates itself to the other treaty parties that it will comply with the terms of the treaty within U.S. territory.

Therefore, the United States needs to take great care when deciding whether to ratify such a treaty when its terms—or the interpretation of those terms by a treaty committee—may not conform to existing state and federal law or to prevalent American social, cultural, and economic norms.

AMERICA'S LEADERSHIP ON DISABILITY RIGHTS

The United States should become party to a treaty only if it advances U.S. national interests. The U.S. should be especially wary of international conventions that require domestic enforcement by the federal government. U.S. national interests in the context of the Convention may be characterized in both foreign and domestic terms: Would becoming a party to the Convention serve U.S. interests within the international community or would joining advance the cause of Americans with disabilities?

From a purely public diplomacy calculus, one can argue that the United States will enhance its reputation within the international community by holding itself to a high standard of human rights. However, in the case of the CRPD, the United States already has effective legislative measures in place to protect the rights of the disabled. Those who say that ratification would allow the United States to claim the moral high ground within the international community—at least in regard to disability rights—imply that the United States is deficient in protecting the rights of the disabled. In truth, the United States has been a leader in protecting the rights of the disabled. It already holds the moral high ground. Signing a treaty merely to "score points" overseas is not a sound basis for making policy.

Ratification of the CRPD is unnecessary to end discrimination against persons with disabilities in the United States. As is made clear throughout the Transmittal Package, the United States already has in place a wide range of federal laws to protect and advance the cause of Americans with disabilities.[8] Major pieces of legislation include the Rehabilitation Act of 1973,[9] the Americans with Disabilities Act (ADA),[10] the Individuals with Disabilities Education Act, Part B,[11] and the Fair Housing Act.[12] Other federal laws that protect persons with disabilities include the Telecommunications Act of 1996, the Air Carrier Access Act of 1986, the Voting Accessibility for the Elderly and Handicapped Act of 1984, the Civil Rights of Institutionalized Persons Act, and the Architectural Barriers Act of 1968.[13]

These federal laws, unlike the broad provisions of the CRPD, were crafted to address the situation of disabled persons living in the United States, not to address the general opinions of the international community. As a whole, the legislation is a firm foundation that can be modified or expanded as necessary through the legislative or regulatory process.

In addition, U.S. disabilities laws are enforced by a panoply of federal agencies, most notably the Civil Rights Division of the Department of Justice.[14] Other elements of the federal government have responsibilities under the ADA and other federal disability legislation. In addition to federal law, all 50 states and the District of Columbia have enacted a wide range of laws to prevent discrimination against the disabled and provide an array of resources to persons with disabilities.[15]

In short, the U.S. government treats disability discrimination in a comprehensive and exhaustive manner that makes membership in an international covenant purporting to set standards for the treatment of the disabled superfluous at best. To allow an international committee of disability experts to scrutinize the U.S. record every four years would yield little or no benefit in realizing disability rights for Americans. Any public diplomacy or other possible marginal benefits, if any, that could arise from ratifying the Convention should be weighed against the negative consequences of ratification.

CEDING AUTHORITY TO AN INTERNATIONAL COMMITTEE

To monitor implementation, human rights treaties usually establish a “committee of experts” to review reports from states parties on their compliance. States parties are required to submit periodic reports (usually every four years) to the committee detailing their compliance with the particular treaty. The CRPD established the Committee on the Rights of Persons with Disabilities (CRPD Committee), which is charged with reviewing periodic reports and making “such suggestions and general recommendations on the report as it may consider appropriate.”[16]

Since the Convention entered into force in May 2008, the CRPD Committee has conducted reviews of a small number of states parties and has issued final conclusions and recommendations regarding Tunisia, Spain and Peru.[17]

Abuses by Treaty Committees. Human rights treaty committees have been known to make demands of states parties that fall well outside the scope of the subject matter of the treaty that conflict with the legal, social, economic, and cultural traditions and norms of states parties. This has especially been the case with the United States.

For instance, in February 2008, the Committee on the Elimination of Racial Discrimination reviewed the U.S. record on racial discrimination and issued a report directing the United States to change its policies on a series of political causes completely divorced from the issues of race and racial discrimination. Specifically, the committee urged the United States to guarantee effective judicial review to the foreign unlawful enemy combatants held at the Guantanamo Bay detention facility, prevent U.S. corporations from abusing the rights of indigenous populations in other countries, place a moratorium on the death penalty, restore voting rights to convicted felons, and other matters completely unrelated or only tangentially related to racial discrimination.[18]

The committees overseeing the enforcement of other human rights treaties to which the United States is not a party often recommend changes in policies that are outside of traditional American norms. For example, the committee that oversees the Convention on the Elimination of All Forms of Discrimination against Women (CEDAW) regularly advocates that states decriminalize prostitution, expand access to abortion, devalue the role of women as mothers, reduce parental authority, and implement strict numerical gender quotas in the government and private sectors.[19]

The U.S. has reason to expect that the experts on the CRPD Committee will give short shrift to U.S. sovereignty, laws, regulations and norms, and embark on similar forays in pursuit of a broader agenda of social engineering unrelated to disability rights.

Defining the CRPD Committee's Role. Any debate over U.S. ratification of the Convention should make it clear through reservations, understandings, and declarations that the CRPD Committee has no power—either through its recommendations or by the issuance of general comments—to provide authoritative or legally enforceable interpretations of the Convention.

The Administrations of Presidents Bill Clinton and George W. Bush held that position regarding human rights treaty committees. For example, in 1994 the Human Rights Committee adopted a general comment which claimed that its "role under the [International] Covenant [on Civil and Political Rights]...necessarily entails interpreting the provisions of the Covenant and the development of a jurisprudence."[20] The Clinton Administration reacted strongly to this claim of authority by issuing a lengthy critique, which stated:

> [The Committee's] rather surprising assertion...would be a rather significant departure from the Covenant scheme, which does not impose on States Parties an obligation to give effect to the Committee's interpretations or confer on the Committee the power to render definitive or binding interpretations of the Covenant. The drafters of the Covenant could have given the Committee this role but deliberately chose not to do so.[21]

The Bush Administration similarly responded to a fact sheet titled "The Right to Health" produced by the Office of the U.N. High Commissioner for Human Rights and the World Health Organization. The fact sheet asserted that the general comments and recommendations adopted by human rights treaty committees "provide an authoritative and detailed interpretation of the provisions found in the treaties."[22] The U.S. response was unequivocal:

> General comments and other documents issued by treaty monitoring bodies express the opinions of individuals acting in their expert capacities; such documents are not the result of deliberations among States. While the views of treaty monitoring bodies are entitled to respect and should be considered carefully by States Parties, they do not create legal obligations or "requirements."[23]

This Committee should be equally clear in reaffirming that the CRPD Committee has no authority to create new international norms or customary international law that the states themselves have not deliberated and approved, particularly any that would arguably bind the U.S. domestically. Such a clarification would reinforce the traditional understanding of customary international law as the "law of nations" that "results from a general and consistent practice of states followed by them from a sense of legal obligation," not from the recommendations of a treaty committee.[24] It would also reaffirm U.S. sovereignty by demonstrating that the federal government will actively work to prevent the improper imposition of norms to which it has not given its democratic consent.[25]

The Committee should also make clear that the CRPD Committee does not possess the authority to dictate the meaning of the Convention to states parties. Its interpretation of the terms of the Convention, the obligations it imposes, and any recommendations and general comments are entitled only to respect and consideration by the member states. The committee should serve a technical, administrative role as opposed to a substantive, adjudicatory, or quasi-lawmaking role. The United States, not a committee of international disability experts, retains the final authority to interpret the terms of the Convention and determine its international obligations.

This Committee has in the past proposed an understanding regarding the authority of a human rights expert committee. Specifically, a Committee report in 2002 proposed the following understanding as a condition to ratification of CEDAW: "Accordingly, the United States understands that the Committee on the Elimination of Discrimination Against Women has no authority to compel actions by States Parties."[26]

NON-SELF-EXECUTION

U.S. ratification of the Convention would make it "the supreme Law of the Land" under the supremacy clause of the Constitution.[27] Although ratification would constitute a commitment under international law, the text of the Convention gives no indication that its drafters intended its provisions to be automatically enforceable under the domestic law of the states parties.[28]

Nevertheless, to protect against any assertion to the contrary and as recommended in the Transmittal Package, this Committee should submit a declaration that the Convention is not self-executing, meaning that its provisions would not be enforceable in U.S. courts. Private causes of action or other new avenues of litigation would thus require passage of federal legislation specifically implementing the Convention's terms.[29]

"Non-self-executing" declarations are common. In fact, the United States has entered such declarations as a condition for ratifying the three major human rights treaties to which it is a party: the International Covenant on Civil and Political Rights (ICCPR),[30] the International Covenant on the Elimination of Racial Discrimination (ICERD),[31] and the Convention Against Torture and Other Cruel, Inhuman or Degrading Treatment or Punishment (CAT).[32] The non-self-executing declaration has also been proposed as a condition for CEDAW ratification.[33]

Of course, the United States would be fully justified in entering such a declaration. Existing state and federal legislation already provide private causes of action for the disabled in the United States, including for instances of discrimination in employment, public accommodations, transportation, telecommunications, housing and other areas.[34]

The Transmittal Package recommends the inclusion of a non-self-executing declaration, but for some reason includes a proviso that "it is not necessary that such Declaration be included in the instrument of ratification deposited by the President."[35] Excluding the declaration would be a departure from U.S. past practice, as the non-self-execution declaration has been included in the U.S. instrument of ratification in connection with the ICCPR, ICERD, and CAT.

"REPRODUCTIVE HEALTH"

For many years there has been a heated debate within the U.N. system regarding abortion "rights."[36] Apparently unwilling to use the term "abortion" in the debate, the proponents of establishing abortion as a human right use phrases such as "reproductive rights" and "sexual and reproductive health" as euphemisms for "abortion rights." The use of one such euphemism in the text of the Convention has extended the abortion debate into the realm of disability rights. Specifically, Article 25 of the Convention requires states parties to "[p]rovide persons with disabilities with the same range, quality and standard of free or affordable health care and programmes as provided to other persons, *including in the area of sexual and reproductive health* and population-based public health programmes."[37]

Within the context of the debate over abortion rights, Article 25 of the Convention could be interpreted as ensuring that persons with disabilities are provided access to free or affordable abortions, assuming such access is provided to non-disabled persons by the state party.

When the U.N. General Assembly approved the final text of the Convention on December 13, 2006, more than one dozen nations, including the United States, made official statements regarding their interpretation of the phrase "reproductive health."[38] The pertinent part of the U.S. statement reads:

> In that regard, the United States understands that the phrase "reproductive health" in subparagraph (a) of article 25 of the draft Convention does not include abortion, and that its use in that article does not create any abortion rights and cannot be interpreted to constitute support, endorsement or promotion of abortion. We stated that understanding at the time of adoption of the Convention in the Ad Hoc Committee, and note that no other delegation suggested a different understanding of that term.[39]

However, that statement conflicts with the opinion of Secretary of State Hillary Clinton regarding the meaning of "reproductive health." On April 22, 2009, Secretary Clinton testified before the House Foreign Affairs Committee,

"We happen to think that family planning is an important part of women's health, and *reproductive health includes access to abortion*, that I believe should be safe, legal and rare."[40]

Due to this apparent conflict in the interpretation of "reproductive health," this Committee should clarify the nature of the Convention regarding that phrase and its relationship to abortion.[41]

Similar issues arose in this Committee in 1994 and 2002 in the context of CEDAW. In these instances, Senators raised the question of whether abortion rights were to be inferred from certain language in CEDAW that related to "family planning." This Committee issued two reports (in 1994 and 2002) submitting understandings that the U.S. will "determine which health care services are appropriate in connection with family planning, pregnancy, confinement and the post-natal period...." Moreover, in the 2002 report the Committee required as a condition to the Senate's advice and consent an understanding explicitly stating that nothing in CEDAW "shall be construed to reflect or create any right to abortion and in no case should abortion be promoted as a method of family planning."[42]

Abortion remains one of the most heated social issues being debated in the United States among activist groups, state and federal legislatures, and courts at all levels, including the U.S. Supreme Court. Introducing an "international" opinion on the matter from a group of disability experts ensconced in Geneva is unlikely to resolve or advance the debate in the United States.

DEFINING THE CONVENTION'S TERMS

It stands to reason that an international treaty designed to end discrimination on the basis of "disability" should provide a working definition of that term, yet the Convention provides none.[43] In fact, the treaty clouds any legally workable definition of disability by stating in its opening paragraphs that "disability is an evolving concept."[44] Such ambiguity invites abuse by persons or groups who do not suffer from a recognized medical disability, yet seek resources and protection under the authority of the Convention. This would also complicate implementation of the Convention in the United States, in which the definition of "disability" is still regularly contested by activists, litigants, and judges.

Under the Americans with Disabilities Act, a person is considered disabled if he has "a physical or mental impairment that substantially limits one or more...major life activities," has "a record of such an impairment," or has been “regarded as having such an impairment.”[45] Recent amendments to the ADA further clarified that definition by defining “major life activities” to include “caring for oneself, performing manual tasks, seeing, hearing, eating, sleeping, walking, standing, lifting, bending, speaking, breathing, learning, reading, concentrating, thinking, communicating, and working” and “[m]ajor bodily functions.”[46]

Absent a definition or an “evolving” definition, ratification may result in conflict between U.S. law and the Convention. The Administration has recognized the potential for conflict between the definitions (or lack thereof) of “disability” and “persons with disabilities” and has recommended an understanding to address the issue.[47]

But that understanding falls short. To ensure that the United States is not seen to consent to other key definitions the understanding should be broadened to include the terms “discrimination based on disability,” “reasonable accommodation,” and “major life activity.” The CRPD Committee may interpret these terms differently than Congress or U.S. courts would interpret them. For instance, a committee of experts recently questioned the United States on whether the definition of “racial discrimination” under U.S. law comported with the terms of the ICERD.[48]

The United States has similarly qualified terminology in previous treaties. For example, when the United States ratified the United Nations Convention Against Torture and Other Cruel, Inhuman or Degrading Treatment or Punishment, it entered an understanding that substituted its own definition of “torture,” which differed from the convention’s definition.[49] The United States also entered a reservation that limited the treaty’s definition of “cruel, inhuman or degrading treatment or punishment” to prohibit only those acts considered cruel, inhuman, or degrading treatment or punishment under the U.S. Constitution.[50]

* * *

U.S. membership in the Convention would produce, at best, an intangible, incalculable, and marginal public diplomacy benefit in the international community. The United States need not become party to the Convention to demonstrate its commitment to the rights of persons with disabilities or to advance the cause of the disabled in other nations. Any nation that questions U.S. dedication to protecting Americans with disabilities need only review the architecture of state and federal laws and the network of state and federal agencies that enforce those laws.

On the domestic front, persons with disabilities in the United States would be better served by a continual review of the implementation of existing state and federal laws. The U.S. Congress, American civil society, and special interest groups are far better positioned to conduct such reviews than a committee of disability experts from Bangladesh, China, Qatar, and Tunisia, which are current members of the CRPD Committee.

In addition to the reservations, understandings, and declarations (RUDs) included in the President's Transmittal Package, this Committee should include additional RUDs in its resolution of advice and consent to ratification. At a minimum, the following RUDs should be made:

- *Definitions.* The Transmittal Package recommends an understanding in regard to the definition of "disability" and "persons with disabilities," but there are several other crucial definitions, including some that are defined by the Convention, that should be addressed. An understanding along the following general lines would make clear that the United States is not obligated to accept the CRPD Committee's interpretation of these terms: *The United States would consider itself bound by the obligations of the Convention only insofar as the terms "disability," "persons with disabilities," "discrimination based on disability," "reasonable accommodation," and "major life activity" are defined coextensively with the definitions of such terms pursuant to the relevant laws in the United States.*
- *The Authority of the CRPD Committee.* An understanding along the following general lines would make clear that the United States considers the role of the Committee on the Rights of Persons with Disabilities to be technical and advisory, as opposed to authoritative or adjudicatory: *The United States understands that the Committee on the Rights of Persons with Disabilities has no authority to compel actions by states parties, and the United States does not consider conclusions, recommendations, or general comments issued by the committee as constituting customary international law or legally binding on it in any manner.*
- *"Reproductive Health".* To remain consistent with the U.S. understanding of the term "reproductive health" at the time that the Convention was adopted in 2006, an understanding along the following lines should be included in the resolution of advice and consent: *The United States understands that the phrase "sexual and*

reproductive health" in Article 25(a) of the Convention does not include abortion, and its use in that Article does not create any abortion rights, and cannot be interpreted to constitute support, endorsement, or promotion of abortion, and in no case should abortion be promoted as a method of family planning.

These RUDs, in addition to those recommended in the Transmittal Package, could limit, although not eliminate, the danger that the Convention would pose to U.S. law and American sovereignty. Regardless, even with the inclusion of the aforementioned RUDs, U.S. ratification will not advance its national interests. Nor will it advance the cause of Americans with disabilities.

Current U.S. law meets or exceeds the provisions of the Convention, and mere membership in the Convention will not convince the international community that America protects the rights of its disabled citizens. Moreover, ratification of the Convention may harm U.S. national interests because human rights treaty committees increasingly view themselves as the legislators of binding international norms, instead of as experts fulfilling the technical roles they were intended to perform.

—Steven Groves is the Bernard and Barbara Lomas Fellow in the Margaret Thatcher Center for Freedom, a division of the Kathryn and Shelby Cullom Davis Institute for International Studies, at The Heritage Foundation.

* * *

The Heritage Foundation is a public policy, research, and educational organization recognized as exempt under section 501(c)(3) of the Internal Revenue Code. It is privately supported and receives no funds from any government at any level, nor does it perform any government or other contract work.

The Heritage Foundation is the most broadly supported think tank in the United States. During 2011, it had nearly 700,000 individual, foundation, and corporate supporters representing every state in the U.S. Its 2011 income came from the following sources:

Individuals 78%Foundations 17%Corporations 5%

The top five corporate givers provided The Heritage Foundation with 2% of its 2011 income. The Heritage Foundation's books are audited annually by the national accounting firm of McGladrey & Pullen. A list of major donors is available from The Heritage Foundation upon request.

Members of The Heritage Foundation staff testify as individuals discussing their own independent research. The views expressed are their own and do not reflect an institutional position for The Heritage Foundation or its board of trustees.

End Notes

[1] Convention on the Rights of Persons with Disabilities, art. 1.
[2] Ibid., arts. 10, 12, 14, and 21
[3] Ibid., arts. 24, 25, and 28.
[4] U.N. Office of Legal Affairs, Treaty Section, "Status: Convention on the Rights of Persons with Disabilities," United Nations Treaty Collection," at http://treaties.un.org/pages/ViewDetails.aspx?src=TREATY&mtdsg_no=IV15&chapter=4&lang=en (July 10, 2012).
[5] Edith M. Lederer, "US Signs Disabled Rights Treaty," ABC News, July 30, 2009, at http://abcnews.go.com/US/wireStory?id=8215921 (April 15, 2010).
[6] Message from the President of the United States transmitting the Convention on the Rights of Persons with Disabilities, 112th Cong., 2nd Sess., Treaty Doc. 112-7, May 17, 2012, at http://www.gpo.gov/fdsys/pkg/CDOC112tdoc7/pdf/CDOC-112tdoc7.pdf (July 10, 2012).
[7] U.S. Constitution, art. VI, cl. 2.
[8] Transmittal Package, Tab 1-2, pp. 83-93.
[9] 29 U.S.C. § 791 et seq.
[10] 42 U.S.C. § 12101 et seq., later amended by the ADA Amendments Act of 2008, Public Law 110–325 (enacted on September 25, 2008).
[11] 20 U.S.C. § 1400 et seq. The Education for All Handicapped Children Act, the predecessor legislation to IDEA, was enacted in 1975.
[12] 42 U.S.C. § 3601 et seq.
[13] 42 U.S.C. §§ 255, 251(a)(2); 49 U.S.C. § 41.705; 42 U.S.C. §§ 1973ee et seq.; 42 U.S.C. §§ 1997 et seq.; 42 U.S.C. §§ 4151 et seq. See also U.S. Department of Justice, Civil Rights Division, Disability Rights Section, "A Guide to Disability Rights Laws," September 2005, at http://www.ada.gov/cguide.htm#anchor64984 (April 15, 2010).
[14] U.S. Department of Justice, Civil Rights Division, "Disability Rights Section Home Page," at http://www.justice.gov/crt/drs/drshome.php (April 15, 2010). See also Americans with Disabilities Act, "ADA Home Page," at http://www.ada.gov (April 15, 2010).
[15] For example, see Cancer Legal Line, "State Disability Discrimination Laws," http://www.marrow.org/PATIENT/Support_Resources/Patient_Teleconferen/PDFs/Aug.6.08.HandoutState_Disability_Laws.pdf (April 15, 2010); Disability.gov, "Information by State," at http://www.disability.gov/state/index (April 15, 2010).
[16] Convention on the Rights of Persons with Disabilities, art. 36(1).
[17] Committee on the Rights of Persons with Disabilities, "Concluding observations," Tunisia, CRPD/C/TUN/CO/1, May 13, 2011, at http://www2.ohchr.org//SPdocs/CRPD/5thsession/CRPD-C-TUN-CO-1_en.doc (July 10, 2012); Spain, CRPD/C/ESP/CO/1, October 19, 2011, at http://www.ohchr.org/Documents/HRBodies/CRPD/ 6thsession/CRPD.C.ESP.CO.1_en.doc (July 10, 2012); Peru, CRPD/C/PER/CO/1, May 9, 2012, at http://www.ohchr.org/Documents/HRBodies/CRPD/7thsession/CRPD.C.PER.CO.1-ENG.doc (July 10, 2012).

The Committee may have completed reports on Argentina, China, and Hungary, but if so the reports are not yet available online.

[18] Steven Groves, "The Inequities of the U.N. Committee on the Elimination of Racial Discrimination," Heritage Foundation Backgrounder No. 2168, August 7, 2008, at http://www.heritage.org/Research/InternationalOrganizations/bg2168.cfm. See also Committee on the Elimination of Racial Discrimination, "Concluding Observations of the Committee on the Elimination of Racial Discrimination: United States of America," CERD/C/USA/CO/6, February 2008, at http://www.universalhumanrightsindex.org/documents/824/1310/document/en/text.html (April 15, 2010).

[19] Patrick F. Fagan, "How U.N. Conventions on Women's and Children's Rights Undermine Family, Religion, and Sovereignty," Heritage Foundation Backgrounder No. 1407, February 5, 2001, at http://www.heritage.org/Research/Reports/2001/02/How-UN-Conventions-On-Womens; Grace Melton, "CEDAW: How U.N. Interference Threatens the Rights of American Women," Heritage Foundation Backgrounder No. 2227, January 9, 2009, at http://www.heritage.org/Research/Reports/2009/01/CEDAW-How-UN-Interference-Threatensthe-Rights-of-American-Women; and Wendy Wright, "CEDAW Committee Rulings," Concerned Women for America, August 27, 2002, at http://www.cwfa.org/articledisplay.asp?id=1870 (April 15, 2010).

[20] U.N. Office of the High Commissioner for Human Rights, "General Comment No. 24: Issues Relating to Reservations Made upon Ratification or Accession to the Covenant or the Optional Protocols Thereto, or in Relation to Declarations Under Article 41 of the Covenant," CCPR/C/21/Rev.1/Add.6, November 4, 1994, at http://www.unhchr.ch/tbs/doc.nsf/(Symbol)/69c55b086f72957ec12563ed004ecf7a (April 15, 2010).

[21] Observations by the Governments of the United States and the United Kingdom on Human Rights Committee General Comment No. 24 (52) relating to reservations, U.N. document A/50/40, p. 1, March 28, 1995, at http://www.iilj.org/courses/documents/USand UK Responses.pdf (April 15, 2010).

[22] Office of the U.N. High Commissioner for Human Rights and World Health Organization, "The Right to Health," Fact Sheet No. 31, June 2008, p. 10, at http://www.ohchr.org/Documents/Publications/Factsheet31.pdf (April 16, 2010).

[23] U.S. Department of State, "Observations by the United States of America on 'The Right to Health, Fact Sheet No. 31,'" October 15, 2008, at http://www.globalgovernancewatch.org/docLib/20081222_Health_USG_Paper.pdf (April 16, 2010).

[24] Restatement (Third) of the Foreign Relations Law of the United States §102(2) (1987), and Curtis A. Bradley and Jack L. Goldsmith, Foreign Relations Law, 2nd ed. (New York: Aspen Publishers, 2006).

[25] For a critique of the "modern position" that customary international law is applicable or enforceable within the United States, see Curtis A. Bradley and Jack L. Goldsmith, "Customary International Law as Federal Common Law: A Critique of the Modern Position," Harvard Law Review, Vol. 110, No. 4 (February 1997), p. 815.

[26] Convention on the Elimination of All Forms of Discrimination Against Women, Senate Exec. Rept. 107–9, 107th Cong., 2nd Sess., September 6, 2002, p. 13. Citing a July 8, 2002, letter from Secretary of State Colin Powell, the report stated, "State Parties have always retained the discretion on whether to implement any recommendations made by the Committee."

[27] "This Constitution, and the Laws of the United States which shall be made in Pursuance thereof; and all Treaties made, or which shall be made, under the Authority of the United States, shall be the supreme Law of the Land; and the Judges in every State shall be bound

thereby, any Thing in the Constitution or Laws of any State to the Contrary notwithstanding." U.S. Constitution, art. VI, cl. 2.

[28] "This Court has long recognized the distinction between treaties that automatically have effect as domestic law, and those that—while they constitute international law commitments—do not by themselves function as binding federal law." Medellin v. Texas, 552 U.S. 491, 504 (2008).

[29] "International agreements, even those directly benefiting private persons, generally do not create private rights or provide for a private cause of action in domestic courts." 2 Restatement (Third) of Foreign Relations Law of the United States § 907, Comment a, p. 395 (1986).

[30] "That the United States declares that the provisions of articles 1 through 27 of the Covenant are not self-executing." International Covenant on Civil and Political Rights, December 16, 1966, in United Nations, Treaty Series, Vol. 999, p. 171 and Vol. 1057, p. 407, "Declarations and Reservations," United States, Declaration (1), at http://treaties.un.org/Pages/ViewDetails.aspx?src=TREATY&mtdsg_no=IV-4&chapter=4&lang=en (April 16, 2010).

[31] "That the United States declares that the provisions of the Convention are not self-executing." International Covenant on the Elimination of Racial Discrimination, Declarations and Reservations, United States, III, at http://treaties.un.org/Pages/ViewDetails.aspx?src=TREATY&mtdsg_no=IV-2&chapter=4&lang=en#EndDec (April 19, 2010).

[32] "That the United States declares that the provisions of articles 1 through 16 of the Convention are not self-executing." Convention Against Torture and Other Cruel, Inhuman or Degrading Treatment or Punishment, New York, 10 December 1984, United Nations, Treaty Series, vol. 1465, p. 85, "Declarations and Reservations," United States, III, at http://treaties.un.org/Pages/ViewDetails.aspx?src=TREATY&mtdsg_no=IV-9&chapter=4&lang=en (April 19, 2010).

[33] "The United States declares that, for purposes of its domestic law, the provisions of the Convention are non-selfexecuting." Convention on the Elimination of All Forms of Discrimination Against Women, Senate Exec. Rept. 107– 9, p. 13, September 6, 2002.

[34] Americans with Disabilities Act (ADA), 42 U.S.C. §§ 12101 et seq.; Rehabilitation Act of 1973, 29 U.S.C. § 794; and ADA Amendments Act of 2008, Public Law 110–325.

[35] Transmittal Package, p. 82.

[36] See Douglas Sylva and Susan Yoshihara, "Rights by Stealth: The Role of UN Human Rights Treaty Bodies in the Campaign for an International Right to Abortion," International Organizations Research Group White Paper No 8, reprinted 2009, at http://www.c-fam.org/docLib/20100126_IORG_W_Paper_Number8FINAL.pdf (April 16, 2010).

[37] Convention on the Rights of Persons with Disabilities, art. 25(a) (emphasis added).

[38] See Susan Yoshihara, "UN Adopts Disabilities Treaty, Many States Reiterate Rejection of Abortion," Catholic Family & Human Rights Institute Friday Fax, December 14, 2006, at http://www.cfam.org/publications/id.492/pub_detail.asp (April 16, 2010).

[39] U.N. General Assembly, 61st Session, 76th plenary meeting, U.N. Doc. A/61/PV.76, December 13, 2006, p. 7 (July 10, 2012).

[40] Hearing, New Beginnings: Foreign Policy Priorities in the Obama Administration, Committee on Foreign Affairs, U.S. House of Representatives, 111th Cong., 1st Sess., April 22, 2009, at http://foreignaffairs.house.gov/schedule.asp?showdate=4/22/2009&adj=4/22/2009 (emphasis added)(April 16, 2010).

[41] Article 10 of CRPD, titled "Right to life," requires that "States Parties reaffirm that every human being has the inherent right to life and shall take all necessary measures to ensure its

effective enjoyment by persons with disabilities on an equal basis with others." This provision is seemingly inconsistent with an interpretation of "reproductive health" that requires access to abortion.

[42] Convention on the Elimination of All Forms of Discrimination Against Women, Senate Exec. Rept. 103-38, 103rd Cong., 2nd Sess., October 3, 1994, and Convention on the Elimination of All Forms of Discrimination Against Women, Senate Exec. Rept. 107–9.

[43] There is no definition of "disability" in the operative definition section of the convention (Article 2 "Definitions"). The failure to reach consensus on the definition of "disability" was the result of a dispute concerning whether the term "disability" should be a medical concept or a social concept. Language describing disability as an "evolving concept" certainly leans towards a more social definition. See Susan Yoshihara, "The Quest for Happiness," in Brett D. Schaefer, ed., ConUNdrum: The Limits of the United Nations and the Search for Alternatives (Lanham, Md.: Rowman & Littlefield Publishers, 2009), p. 182.

[44] Convention on the Rights of Persons with Disabilities, Preamble, ¶(e).

[45] Americans with Disabilities Act, 42 U.S.C. § 12102(2).

[46] Public Law 110–325, § 4(a)(2)(A) (September 25, 2008).

[47] Transmittal Package, p. 8.

[48] The CERD Committee rapporteur questioned the U.S. definition of racial discrimination in regard to the necessity to prove intentional discrimination versus practices that are facially neutral but have an unlawful disparate impact upon members of a protected class. Committee on the Elimination of Racial Discrimination, "Questions Put by the Rapporteur in Connection with the Consideration of the Combined Fourth, Fifth and Sixth Periodic Reports of the United States of America (CERD/C/USA/6)," March 7, 2008, pp. 13–15, at http://www.state.gov/documents/organization/107362.pdf (April 19, 2010).

[49] Convention Against Torture and Other Cruel, Inhuman or Degrading Treatment or Punishment, December 10, 1984, in United Nations, Treaty Series, Vol. 1465, p. 85, "Declarations and Reservations," United States, II(1), at http://treaties.un.org/Pages/ViewDetails.aspx?src=TREATY&mtdsg_no=IV-9&chapter=4&lang=en (April 19, 2010).

[50] Ibid., I(1).

In: The United Nations Convention ...
Editor: Timo Wallner ISBN: 978-1-62808-120-6

Chapter 7

TESTIMONY OF MICHAEL FARRIS, CHANCELLOR, PATRICK HENRY COLLEGE. HEARING ON "CONVENTION ON THE RIGHTS OF PERSONS WITH DISABILITIES"*

United States Senate
Foreign Relations Committee
against the United Nations Convention
on the Rights of Persons with Disabilities

Mr. Chairman, thank you for the honor of being invited to testify before this Committee.

My name is Michael Farris. I am the Chancellor of Patrick Henry College where I teach Constitutional Law, Public International Law, and coach our six-time national champion moot court team. I earned my Juris Doctorate from Gonzaga University back in 1976 and my LL.M. in Public International Law just last year from the University of London. I am also the Chairman and Founder of the Home School Legal Defense Association—the largest homeschooling advocacy group in the world.

There are three categories of arguments that I bring in support of the view that the United States Senate should not ratify the UN Convention on the Rights of Persons With Disabilities.

* This is an edited, reformatted and augmented version of testimony given on July 12, 2012 before the Senate Foreign Relations Committee.

1) The promises made by the supporters of the treaty concerning the impact both on Americans and on disabled persons in other countries are clearly false and callously misleading.
2) The changes to American law that will be required to comply with the provisions of this treaty are profound and utterly unacceptable. Specifically, the changes regarding the rights of parents who have children with disabilities—which includes thousands of homeschooling families—are absolutely inconsistent with the IDEA and the basic constitutional principles of parental rights.
3) The ratification of this treaty would constitute the most dangerous departure from the principles of American sovereignty and personal liberty in the history of the United States Senate.

THE PROPONENTS OF THIS TREATY MAKE FALSE AND MISLEADING PROMISES

The advocates of this UN treaty promise two kinds of alluring benefits that will supposedly result from Senate ratification. First, it will help disabled Americans travelling abroad. Second, it will give the United States greater moral authority to coax unwilling states into appropriate treatment of disabled persons within such states.

Neither of these claims have any foundation in law or in fact.

Let me explain why I take these false and misleading claims quite personally.

My mother has had Multiple Sclerosis for over forty years. I have had the honor of pushing my mother's wheel chair through the halls of Congress as well as through museums, castles, and cathedrals in Switzerland, Austria, and France. There is no doubt that the United States leads the whole world in providing appropriate access to persons with disabilities.

We lead—not because international law has required us to do so— rather; we lead because in the United States we believe that every single person is endowed by our Creator with certain inalienable rights. And it is that belief system, and not international law, which will continue to provide Americans with disabilities with any necessary changes to the law in the years ahead.

I deeply resent the attempt by the advocates of this treaty to mislead members of the disabled community with the false promise that the U.S.

ratification of this treaty will lead to material improvements when Americans with disabilities travel to other nations.

U.S. ratification of this treaty creates absolutely no rights for Americans with disabilities when they travel abroad. It is an utterly false contention. If the United States becomes party to a treaty, all of the legal consequences which flow from this act of ratification will be limited to the territory of the United States. There are no extraterritorial rights created for American travelers, businessmen, service members, or veterans.

This is the nature of this kind of treaty. See, Article 29, *Vienna Convention on the Law of Treaties.* It is a promise from the state party to change its own laws and practices so that disabled persons will have greater access and equality.

If an American were traveling in Portugal, for example, he or she would receive no claim whatsoever to improved access from Portugal by virtue of American ratification of this treaty. Portugal's obligation to disabled persons arises from Portugal's own ratification of this treaty—assuming that it lives up to its obligation to enact compliant domestic law.

It is equally disingenuous to claim that U.S. ratification will lead to improved treatment for disabled persons from other countries. This is especially true in light of the package of reservations that the State Department proposes.

The proponents of this treaty, together with the proposed reservations, are attempting to lead the Senate to believe that the United States is already fully compliant with this convention.

Professor Louis Henkin writing in the American Journal of International Law criticizes this approach:

> Reservations designed to reject any obligation to rise above existing law and practice are of dubious propriety: if states generally entered such reservations, the convention would be futile. The object and purpose of the human rights conventions, it would seem, are to promote respect for human rights by having countries—mutually—assume legal obligations to respect and ensure recognized rights in accordance with international standards. Even friends of the United States have objected that its reservations are incompatible with that object and purpose and are therefore invalid.
>
> ... By adhering to human rights conventions subject to these reservations, the United States, it is charged, is pretending to assume international obligations but in fact is undertaking nothing.[1]

In light of this approach, the United States will not be sending any kind of signal worth sending. The message will not be that other nations need to match our comprehensive package of state and federal laws concerning the proper treatment of disabled persons. Rather, the message will be that treaties are for show and have no more impact than you want them to have.

The United States should lead the world in only ratifying treaties with which we intend to fully, faithfully, and vigorously comply. We should not lead the world in cheap and compromised promises.

The fact that no sensible person would dare to suggest that we ratify this treaty without this class of reservations is proof that this treaty is simply too dangerous to ratify.

The way for the United States to continue to lead the world in this area is to ensure that American law and practice live up to the promises of the Declaration of Independence rather than the amorphous standards of a committee of 18 experts in Geneva.

International law that is not translated into domestic law and practice is nearly worthless.

If International Law actually led to greater rights for the citizens of other nations, then why are North Koreans still deprived of any semblance of any human right? That nation has ratified five major human rights treaties and enforces none of them.

Why do Germany and Sweden ban homeschooling and persecute and harass homeschooling parents despite their ratification of human rights treaties which promise that the rights of parents to choose alternatives to public education are prior to the claims of the state?

How has American leadership and example in ratifying human rights instruments led to any help for German or Swedish homeschoolers? In fact, this administration is seeking to deport a German homeschooling family that was awarded asylum by an administrative law judge. What has America done of any substance to help those in the concentration camps of North Korea?

Leadership comes not from ratification of treaties—it comes from effective action. Human rights treaties are empty promises that the do little more than guarantee the right of a professional class of international bureaucrats to full employment and their right to travel to conferences where they shake their heads and ultimately write a report in diplomatic code that does little good for anyone at all.

U.S. ratification of this treaty has no extra-territorial application for our citizens whatsoever. It is a fraudulent charade to claim otherwise.

THIS TREATY REQUIRES RADICAL CHANGES TO AMERICAN LAW

The most basic rule of international law is *pacta sunt servanda*—agreements must be kept. Ratification of the UNCRPD requires the United States to act in good faith—and to conform our law to the standards set forth in this UN treaty.

The proposed declaration that this treaty is non-self-executing does not change this duty in any way. Such a declaration simply removes the possibility of direct judicial imposition of the provisions of the treaty. The United States has made a solemn promise that we *will* change our statutory law to conform to the requirements of the treaty. If we fail to do so, we are in breach of our international legal obligations.

I want to focus on one area of the required changes in American law—the impact that the UNCRPD would have on the rights of parents concerning the education of their disabled and special needs children.

The UNCRPD follows the trend of the second generation of human rights treaties which promote the idea that government, not parents, have the ultimate voice in decisions concerning their children.

Early human rights instruments were very supportive of the rights of parents to direct the education and upbringing of their children.

It is beyond dispute that the Universal Declaration of Human Rights, adopted in 1948 by the unanimous vote of the UN General Assembly arose "out of the desire to respond forcefully to the evils perpetrated by Nazi Germany."[2] The UDHR's view regarding parents and children is no exception to this rule. Article 26(3) of the UDHR proclaims: "Parents have a prior right to choose the kind of education that shall be given to their children." Numerous human rights instruments have been drafted in reaction to "the intrusion of the fascist state into the family...."[3]

The rejection of the Nazi view of parents and children was translated from the aspirational articles of the UDHR into the binding provisions of the two core human rights treaties of our era—the International Covenant on Civil and Political Rights (1966) and the International Covenant on Economic, Social, and Cultural Rights (1966). Article 18(4) of the ICCPR provides:

> The States Parties to the present Covenant undertake to have respect for the liberty of parents and, when applicable, legal guardians to ensure the religious and moral education of their children in conformity with their own convictions.

Article 13(3) of the ICESCR repeats and expands on this same theme:

> The States Parties to the present Covenant undertake to have respect for the liberty of parents and, when applicable, legal guardians to choose for their children schools, other than those established by the public authorities, which conform to such minimum educational standards as may be laid down or approved by the State and to ensure the religious and moral education of their children in conformity with their own convictions.

This pro-parent view of human rights has given way to a decidedly different view in the UN Convention on the Rights of the Child (UNCRC) and now in the UN Convention on the Rights of Persons with Disabilities.

The UNCRPD incorporates several key elements from the UNCRC that, as I will demonstrate, lead to the conclusion that parental rights in the education of disabled children are supplanted by a new theory of governmental oversight and superiority. In short, government agents, and not parents, are being given the authority to decide all educational and treatment issues for disabled children. All of the rights that parents have under both traditional American law and the Individuals with Disabilities Education Act will be undermined by this treaty.

Article 7 is the key. Sections 2 and 3 directly parallel provisions of the UNCRC.

2) In all actions concerning children with disabilities, the best interests of the child shall be a primary consideration.
3) States Parties shall ensure that children with disabilities have the right to express their views freely on all matters affecting them, their views being given due weight in accordance with their age and maturity, on an equal basis with other children, and to be provided with disability and age-appropriate assistance to realize that right.

Section 2 directly parallels Article 2(1) of the CRC. Section 3 closely follows Article 12(1) of the CRC.

The "best interest of the child" standard is a familiar one to anyone who has ever participated in family or juvenile law in American courts. However, in that context it is a dispositional standard. This means that after a parent has been convicted of abusing or neglecting their child, then and only then can the government substitute its view of what it best for the child for that of the parent. Or in the divorce context, once a judge determines the family unit is broken, the judge must settle the contest between the competing parents and decide for herself what she thinks is in the best interest of the child.

In an intact family, where there is no proof of abuse or neglect, government agents—whether school officials, social workers, or judges—cannot substitute their judgment of what is best for a child over the objection of the parents.

This legal principle is firmly imbedded into the Individuals with Disabilities Education Act. Parents have a great deal of authority concerning the education and treatment of their children under this act.

The National Dissemination Center for Children with Disabilities lists eight particular rights of parents contained in the IDEA[4]:

> The right of parents to receive a complete explanation of all the procedural safeguards available under IDEA and the procedures in the state for presenting complaints
>
> Confidentiality and the right of parents to inspect and review the educational records of their child
>
> The right of parents to participate in meetings related to the identification, evaluation, and placement of their child, and the provision of FAPE (a free appropriate public education) to their child
>
> The right of parents to obtain an independent educational evaluation (IEE) of their child
>
> The right of parents to receive "prior written notice" on matters relating to the identification, evaluation, or placement of their child, and the provision of FAPE to their child
>
> The right of parents to give or deny their consent before the school may take certain action with respect to their child
>
> The right of parents to disagree with decisions made by the school system on those issues
>
> The right of parents and schools to use IDEA's mechanisms for resolving disputes, including the right to appeal determinations

I have litigated an additional right of parents under the IDEA—the right to pursue private and home education at one's own expense.

For example, in the Eighth Circuit case of *Fitzgerald v. Camdenton R-III School Dist.*, 439 F.3d 773 (8t[h] Cir. 2006), the court reinforced important parental rights concepts. "[T]he IDEA allows parents to decline services and waive all benefits under the IDEA. See 20 U.S.C. § 1414(a)(1)(D)(ii)(II). When parents waive their child's right to services, school districts may not override their wishes. See *id.*" Id. at 775.

In that case, we contended that parents did not even have to agree to allow the school district to force the child to go through the initial IDEA evaluation. The evidence showed that this homeschooling family had already had their child independently evaluated and the child was receiving private special needs services at the parents' own expense. The school district wanted to force the family to undergo its special needs evaluation even though the school recognized that it could not force this family to accept the recommended services at the end of the process.

The Eighth Circuit ruled for the family saying that the school could not compel this IDEA evaluation under these circumstances.

All of these parental rights will be eviscerated by the mandatory application of the "best interest of the child" standard which is set forth in Article 7 of the UNCRPD.

Geraldine van Bueren, who is one of the world's leading experts on the international rights of the child and helped to draft the UNCRC (and was one of my professors at the University of London), clearly explains the meaning and application of this best interests standard in her course material.

> Best interests provides decision and policy makers with the authority to substitute their own decisions for either the child's or the parents', providing it is based on considerations of the best interests of the child.[5]

Section 7 of the UNCRPD uses the exact same legal terms as those contained in the UNCRC.

Accordingly, today, under the IDEA parents get to decide what they think is best for their child—including the right to walk away from government services and provide private or home education. Under the UNCRPD, that right is supplanted with the rule announced by Professor van Bueren. Government officials have the authority to substitute their views for the views of parents as well as the views of the child as to what is best. If parents think that private schools are best for their child, the UNCRPD gives the government the authority and the legal duty to override that judgment and keep the child in the government-approved program that the officials think is best for the child.

Ask virtually any parent who has dealt with school officials in the IDEA context: Are you willing to give the government the final say on what it thinks is best for your child's special needs or disability?

School districts have a powerful motivation to do better for disabled and special needs children precisely because they know that parents with real rights are looking over their every move and have the ability to fight for what that parent knows to be best for their child. Remove parental authority and institutional lethargy will take over in many cases.

Children are treated much, much better in the special needs setting whenever their parents have real and certain rights.

Those rights are gone if this Senate ratifies this treaty. There are two reasons this is true.

First, virtually every state has state law provisions which also give parents a number of rights in the educational setting. Article VI of the U.S. Constitution contains our Supremacy Clause which explicitly states that a ratified treaty is the Supreme Law of the land and all state law provisions which conflict with the treaty are overridden by the treaty.

Any and all parental rights provisions in state education laws will be void by the direct application of Article 7 of this treaty. Government—not parents— has the authority to decide what is best for children.

Second, we must analyze the impact of the ratification of this treaty based on the presumption that we are going to comply with the treaty in good faith. Accordingly, even with the presumption of the non-self-executing nature of the treaty, if the Senate ratifies this treaty, Congress will have the duty to revise the IDEA to comply with the provisions of the UNCRPD. Therefore, unless we intend to breach our international legal obligations, Congress will be required to modify the IDEA to ensure that government decision-makers, and not parents, have the final say as to what they believe is best for a child.

Thousands of homeschooling parents have children with special needs and disabilities. The ratification of this treaty is considered by our community to be the equivalent of an act of utter betrayal.

As other parents of special needs children come to understand the meaning of these phrases in the UNCRPD, they too will be aghast to learn that this Senate is giving serious consideration to a legally binding international agreement that would undermine their rights as American parents.

No proposed reservation can cure this problem. And unless we adopt a reservation that explicitly says: *We are not serious about any duty to comply with this treaty and are ratifying only for PR purposes*—I can think of no means of drafting a reservation that cures this huge defect.

Here is the plain fact. American law and international law are not compatible when it comes to parental rights. I can think of no good reason why we should even try. Americans should make the law for America—we do not need a committee of experts in Geneva to look over our shoulders to help us determine what kind of policy we need to best protect Americans with special needs and disabilities.

Although there are a great number of other difficulties that are latent in this treaty, I want to focus just on one other issue. This treaty appears to take sides on the public policy issues concerning abortion.

Article 25(a) of the UNCRPD requires state parties to:

> Provide persons with disabilities with the same range, quality and standard of free or affordable health care and programmes as provided to other persons, including in the area of sexual and reproductive health and population-based public health programmes;

This provision has led the nations of Poland, Malta, and Monaco to adopt reservations or declarations that proclaim that these states do not recognize any right to an abortion or mandatory state-funding for the same.

Under *Roe v. Wade*, of course, we live under a regime where it is proclaimed that women have the constitutional right to abortion. There is great controversy over that decision—and Congress has generally avoided federal funding for abortion. It would reasonably appear that Article 25(a) commits the United States to providing free abortion services to persons with disabilities. A vote for this treaty is a vote for abortion funding.

Of course, our State Department has not proposed anything like the reservations from Poland, Malta, or Monaco. And I doubt that the omission was a mere oversight.

This Treaty Would Violate the Principles of American Sovereignty and Liberty

The Founders of this Republic understood treaties to be exclusively devoted to the subject matter of how nations treat other nations. The idea that international law would be used to dictate the policies that our nation would follow concerning the rights of our own citizens would, frankly, astonish and bewilder the founding generation.

In the most basic terms, American sovereignty means that Americans should make the law for America. No foreign power should have the ability to lay claim to a power to dictate what our internal domestic law should be.

This treaty would alter that balance. I return to Professor van Bueren for an explanation of the impact on sovereignty by the ratification of this kind of treaty. Although her comments were directed toward the ratification of the UNCRC, they are fully applicable here.

> Underpinning this approach are the legal consequences of states becoming party to the Convention on the Rights of the Child. The United Nations Convention on the Rights of the Child moves the borders for the state of what is political and what can be subject to a legal challenge in courts, particularly in resource allocation and budgetary matters. The Convention and other international laws in effect narrows what were previously unfettered discretionary powers of governments. Before governments become party to human rights treaty they are obliged to ensure that there are the resources, either to implement the Convention on becoming party or shortly thereafter, in accordance with international law. Hence, there is no interference with national sovereignty, the nationally sovereign decisions on how resources on children's rights to be expended have already been taken. In essence, the government has exercised its political powers, and it has to live with the legal consequences.[6]

There is a once for all decision that effectively exhausts our sovereignty. If we ratify this treaty, our ability to have absolute freedom of choice concerning our public policy on this subject has been extinguished. It is akin to the states being under a federal mandate. Sure, the states have a bit of discretion in how the federal mandate will be implemented, but their range of policy choices are circumscribed by the duty to implement the will of Congress. In a similar fashion, if the Senate ratifies this treaty—the nationally sovereign decisions will be made once for all. Generations of Americans will be forced to live with this decision—under a permanent duty to live under UN supervision for compliance with our international legal obligations.

There is a second, more specific problem with this particular treaty.

Human rights treaties in general seek to guarantee five sectors of rights—political, civil, economic, social, and cultural rights. The Universal Declaration of Human Rights (which was a statement of altruism and not binding international law) encompassed all five of these components of international law.

However, in the years that followed, there was a great division between two sectors of human rights. Political and civil rights are called negative rights. These rights are what government cannot do to us or take from us. The United States Bill of Rights is the world's greatest collection of negative rights.

However, economic, social, and cultural rights are called positive rights. These rights encompass services that the government must provide its citizens—the right to health care, the right to food, the right to employment.

When the UN attempted to translate the UDHR into formal treaty language—this divide between civil and political rights vs. economic, social, and cultural rights took center stage. The west, led by the United States, supported the creation and ratification of civil and political rights. The Soviet Union and its allies, however, opposed civil and political rights and instead urged the creation of economic, social, and cultural rights.

The attempt to create a single treaty encompassing all of the principles of the UDHR failed. Instead, the UN promulgated two separate treaties—the International Covenant on Civil and Political Rights and the International Covenant on Economic, Social, and Cultural Rights.

The United States ratified the ICCPR. The Soviet Union ratified the ICESCR.

To this very day, the United States has never ratified a UN human rights treaty that has economic, social, and cultural rights at the core of the treaty.

Why is this? Professor van Bueren explains:

> The essence of economic and social, and to an extent, cultural rights is that they involve redistribution, a task with which, despite the vision of human rights, most constitutional courts and regional and international tribunals are distinctively uncomfortable.[7]

Like these courts, the United States Senate—up until this present time—has shared this concern about committing our nation to the task of redistribution.

This treaty would break all precedent of this body. It would be the first time in the history of the Senate that the United States commits itself to a treaty that requires the redistribution of the resources of Americans. We must take resources from some Americans and give them to other Americans.

There is little wonder that the Union of Soviet Socialist Republics favored this kind of redistributive right. But, up until today, the United States Senate has never ratified a treaty embracing these so-called positive rights which are nothing more than the international entitlement to the redistribution of resources.

You may call it what you will. I see such treaties as a dramatic loss of American freedom in favor of coercive international socialism.

CONCLUSION

It was American self-government and not international law that led to the significant advancements that this nation has seen in the appropriate law and policies concerning persons with disabilities.

International law has no track record of success that could lead any reasonable person to believe that international law would have any claim of superiority over American self-government.

We should pass whatever laws we need to ensure proper policies and practices for Americans with disabilities. But we should not give away our policy prerogatives to the superintendence of a committee of UN experts sitting in Geneva.

End Notes

[1] Louis Henkin, *U.S. Ratification of Human Rights Conventions: The Ghost of Senator Bricker*, The American Journal of International Law, Vol 89 No 2, 343-344 (Apr. 1995).

[2] Kathleen Renee Cronin-Furman, "60 Years of the Universal Declaration of Human Rights: Towards an Individual Responsibility to Protect," 25 Am. U. Int'l L. Rev. 175, 176 (2009).

[3] Marleen Eijkholt, "The Right to Found a Family as a Stillborn Right to Procreate?" 18 Med. L. Rev. 127, 134 (2010).

[4] http://nichcy.org/schoolage/parental-rights

[5] Geraldine Van Bueren, *International Rights of the Child, Section D* University of London, 46 (2006).

[6] Geraldine Van Bueren, *International Rights of the Child, Section D*, University of London, 36 (2006).

[7] Geraldine Van Bueren, *Combating Child Poverty—Human Rights Approaches*, Human Rights Quarterly, Vol. 21, p. 680, 680-681 (1999).

In: The United Nations Convention … ISBN: 978-1-62808-120-6
Editor: Timo Wallner

Chapter 8

TESTIMONY OF JOHN LANCASTER, RETIRED EXECUTIVE DIRECTOR, NATIONAL COUNCIL ON INDEPENDENT LIVING. HEARING ON "CONVENTION ON THE RIGHTS OF PERSONS WITH DISABILITIES"*

Senator Kerry, Senator Lugar, and Members of the Foreign Relations Committee, thank you for the opportunity to testify on behalf of American veterans and civilians with disabilities on an issue extremely important to us, the Convention on the Rights of Persons with Disabilities. As a disabled veteran, I join 21 veterans service organizations and over 165 disability organizations in supporting the CRPD. I respectfully request that you support U.S. ratification of this disability treaty and move it to a floor vote in the Senate.

Let me provide some background on my career and experience. I have served the U.S. in a variety of capacities. First, as a Second Lieutenant in the Marine Corps during the Vietnam War, then as an attorney for the Board of Veterans Appeals, and later as an Executive assistant to the Chairman and then Executive Director of the President's Committee on Employment of People with Disabilities. I am currently a Board Member of the U.S. Institute of Peace. As a private citizen, I have also served as the Executive Director for the National Council on Independent Living, worked with Paralyzed Veterans of

* This is an edited, reformatted and augmented version of a testimony presented July 12, 2012 before the Senate Foreign Relations Committee.

America, and sit on the boards of Handicap International, the United States International Council on Disabilities and the World Institute on Disability.

As you can likely surmise, I have focused my entire career on the rights of people with disabilities. My firsthand experience with disability was early in my youth. I was commissioned a Second Lieutenant in the Marine Corps upon graduation from the University of Notre Dame and the Naval ROTC program in June 1967. After additional training, I had orders to Vietnam. I joined the Marine Corps because of a firm belief in the liberty, freedom and opportunity our United States Constitution ensures. I believed then, as I do now, in our responsibility to serve our great country and what, at its best, we represent to all mankind. In 1968, I arrived in Vietnam during the Tet Offensive, assigned to the 1st Battalion, 27th Marines as an Infantry Platoon Commander. Five months later, I was shot and injured in a firefight. After months of rehabilitation, I arrived back home in Western New York a disabled veteran. Although my friends and family welcomed me home, society did not receive me quite as well. While there was certainly tension around the politics of the Vietnam War, it was the inaccessibility of my environment that made me feel the least welcome. I returned to a country not ready to receive me as a man who now used a wheelchair. Let me give you some examples. Buses were not equipped for wheelchair users, neither were trains. Airline companies at the time did not want to deal with wheelchairs. Most buildings, including government buildings, were not accessible. I experienced denial of the simplest pleasures such as going to a restaurant with my family. Even my own alma mater wanted to deny me the opportunity to advance my education. When I applied for law school at Notre Dame, I was told that although I qualified they could not accept me because the school was inaccessible. It was only when I agreed to make my own arrangements and bring my own chair that they accepted me. I graduated in 1974 with a law degree in spite of these unfortunate barriers. The employment discrimination I experienced as a young attorney was unbelievable. The only ones who would hire me were the VA's Board of Veterans Appeals.

For many years, I struggled with needless environmental obstacles and barriers ever-present in my daily life. That is, until the U.S. enacted, in what I believe one of its proudest moments, the Americans with Disabilities Act under President George H.W. Bush. This law led the way for people with disabilities to be accepted in society. It removed people from isolation and segregation, and allowed us to enjoy the fruits of our country with our family and friends without having to bear the shame and stigma of being born with or having acquired a disability. In 1991, a year after the ADA passed, I had the pleasure to serve as an assistant to Justin Dart, the Chairman of the President's Committee on Employment of People with Disabilities under the George H.W. Bush Administration. When President Clinton assumed presidency, the Committee's new Chair, Tony Coelho, appointed me as the Executive Director. In my nine years with the Committee, I traveled to every state in the country several times assisting business and government leaders in the ADA's implementation. I witnessed the historic changes brought about by the ADA. I can tell you that today our returning service members with disabilities are welcomed home to a country that will not deny them any opportunity or freedom. As President George H.W. Bush had intended, this law crumbled the shameful walls of exclusion. I am so pleased to see that that President Bush is an advocate for the CRPD and is able to now see the global impact that this law is making twenty-two years later.

I tell this story of the ADA in our country because it is the movement of the United States disability community that has sprouted similar movements abroad and has inspired this global treaty that we are here to discuss today. The American disability community as a whole worked tirelessly to see the ADA passed, including veterans, the deaf community, people with developmental disabilities, and parents of people with disabilities. Following its enactment, we saw an incredible rise in the development of disability civil society abroad taking similar action to achieve their rights. As we all began to work together and informally share ideas and experiences, we decided that it was time for a global framework that would pave the way for a world that would protect the dignity and freedom of people with disabilities. The U.S. disability community was eager to participate.

In 2001, the drafting of the Convention on the Rights of Persons with Disabilities began. Civil society contributed in an unprecedented way. Many of those in the room with us today were part of the disability community weighing in on the key principles of this important treaty.

Drawing from the ADA, the CRPD seeks to ensure that people with disabilities are accepted in society, receive reasonable accommodations (a concept invented by the United States), and are guaranteed options for community living and rights to a family life. The adoption of the treaty in 2006 was an incredible accomplishment and has led to the development of disability rights around the world. For the record, let me name a few. Kenya, who ratified the treaty in 2008, worked to specifically include the rights of persons with disabilities in their new 2010 constitution. Nigeria, a country that has a history of serious discrimination against children with albinism, has created a ministerial committee on albinism since their ratification of the treaty in 2010. Moldova, who also ratified in 2010, is currently using the CRPD to develop a roadmap for new methods to approach disability domestically with a particular focus on de-institutionalization. The United Arab Emirates, since ratifying the CRPD, has enacted a new law that focuses on promoting positive attitudes towards disability and improving building codes to provide accessibility. These are just a few examples, but the reality is that the CRPD is beginning to have a significant impact around the world.

If the United States has accomplished so much then why ratify, you might ask. For one, I believe that U.S. participation on treaty implementation will yield even more progress and will offer the expertise and technical knowledge that many of these countries do not have in the area of disability rights. From a veteran perspective, I think we have much to gain from the improved accessibility of the world. Today, some disabled soldiers and Marines remain on active duty in-spite of their disability, continuing to serve their country. These service members should be afforded the same rights outside the United States as they enjoy here. For a disabled veteran working abroad, the adoption of disability rights and implementation of disability laws allows them to do their jobs more effectively and reaffirms what they served for: liberty and the opportunity to participate. Let me add, that I speak also for the many service members and veterans abroad who travel with their children with disabilities. A more accessible environment in the countries where they are stationed will no doubt serve these children well. Many veterans, like myself, are engaged in international work in some capacity. From 2000 to 2004, I worked in Hanoi as an advisor to the Vietnamese Government on disability law, policy and programs. The project was funded by the US Agency for International Development. In Hanoi, accessible transportation was rare so I would hold onto a cyclo, a bicycle rickshaw, to get around. Following their signature of the CRPD in 2007, Vietnam began planning for an accessible rapid bus system in Hanoi. This system is now under development. The CRPD is a wonderful tool to help ensure the sustainability of US AID dollars spent overseas on disability related issues while also expanding access for veterans with disabilities, like myself, who choose to work in these countries.

Veterans with disabilities have contributed to the American disability movement in many ways, including through participation in sport and recreation. This has destroyed stereotypes and created positive messages about equality, dignity and worth. Accessibility is a major challenge for American athletes with disabilities during these international trips. From being compelled to deal with air travel regulations that force them to sit in the back of an airplane and crawl to the aircraft bathroom, to pilots who refuse to take them or their gear onboard, to hotel accommodations that have limited or no accessibility, to competition facilities with inaccessible bathrooms, showers, and locker rooms – American athletes face countless discriminatory and inaccessible obstacles abroad.

Despite these challenges, the 2012 Paralympic Games later this summer demonstrates the growth and interest in sport for athletes with disabilities. As this Committee considers this treaty the world will be turning their eyes to London for both the Olympics and Paralympics. The International Paralympic Committee has confirmed that 165 countries - 19 more than in Beijing four years ago – will send more than 4,200 competitors to the Games making it the largest Paralympic competition to date. The U.S., a leader in sport for people with disabilities, sends one of the largest teams, and our athletes are some of the best trained and coached in the world. This year's delegation will also feature many new athletes with disabilities - veterans and active duty service men and women – who are finding success competing in Paralympic sport. Regrettably they are subjected to the same inhospitable conditions created by the lack of accessibility in the international travel and sporting environments found in other countries. As we send our teams off this summer, and celebrate their success in international competition, we should do so with a favorable vote on the CRPD behind us. Ratification of the CRPD is a must for the U.S. to remain competitive since our athletes must compete in international competitions to obtain and maintain their international rankings.

These are just a few examples of why it is in the United States interest to ratify the CRPD. As the treaty package presented to the Senate reveals, the U.S. has an incomparable set of laws that protect the rights of people with disabilities. Looking around this room today, you can see the prosthetics, wheelchairs, software and communications technologies developed by the United States. As more countries ratify at an unprecedented pace, the need for accessible devices and software steadily increases for people with disabilities around the world. Many of these products are engineered, manufactured, or sold by U.S. corporations that can meet these new demands. Indeed, the CRPD is good for all American businesses. It will level the playing field for foreign businesses. They will now have to comply with the employment rights and the accommodation requirements that US businesses already meet. The United States has valuable information to share with the rest of the world, not only for the benefit of the world's 1 billion people with disabilities, but specifically for the 54 million people with disabilities who may wish to work, serve, study, and travel abroad. In 2012, 22 years after the passage of the Americans with

Disabilities Act, it is unacceptable that many Americans with disabilities cannot leave the borders of the United States without the fear of stigma, barriers, and denial of their rights.

Ratifying the CRPD costs nothing, will require no changes in law, and provides us the leadership opportunity to effectively guide a framework for countries to advance and sustain disability rights in their own country. Not joining this treaty, however, comes with a grave cost: the inability of the U.S. to participate and the loss of an opportunity to take a stand for what's right. 42 years after I served our country in Vietnam, I still believe in the same principles of why I first enlisted: I stand behind a firm belief in the liberty and freedom we enjoy in the United States and our responsibility to serve and participate. I am proud of this country and our laws and I urge you, on behalf of 21 veterans service organizations and 165 disability organizations, to support ratification of this treaty so that we can participate and continue America's noble history of leadership. Thank you.

In: The United Nations Convention …
Editor: Timo Wallner
ISBN: 978-1-62808-120-6

Chapter 9

THE AMERICANS WITH DISABILITIES ACT (ADA): STATUTORY LANGUAGE AND RECENT ISSUES*

Cynthia Brougher and James V. DeBergh

SUMMARY

The Americans with Disabilities Act (ADA) provides broad nondiscrimination protection in employment, public services, public accommodations, services operated by public entities, transportation, and telecommunications for individuals with disabilities. This report summarizes the major provisions of the ADA and analyzes selected recent issues, including the Supreme Court cases and the ADA Amendments Act of 2008.

BACKGROUND

The Americans with Disabilities Act, ADA, 42 U.S.C. §§12101 *et seq.*, has often been described as the most sweeping nondiscrimination legislation

* This is an edited, reformatted and augmented version of the Congressional Research Service Publication, CRS Report for Congress 98-921, dated March 22, 2012.

since the Civil Rights Act of 1964. It provides broad nondiscrimination protection in employment, public services, public accommodations, and services operated by private entities, transportation, and telecommunications for individuals with disabilities.[1] As stated in the act, its purpose is "to provide a clear and comprehensive national mandate for the elimination of discrimination against individuals with disabilities." Enacted on July 26, 1990, the majority of the ADA's provisions took effect in 1992.[2] The ADA Amendments Act, P.L. 110-325, was enacted on September 25, 2008, to respond to a series of Supreme Court decisions that had interpreted the definition of disability narrowly.[3]

The Supreme Court has decided 20 ADA cases.[4] In the most recent Supreme Court decision, *United States v. Georgia,*[5] the Court held that Title II of the ADA created a private cause of action for damages against the states for conduct that actually violated the Fourteenth Amendment. However, the Court did not reach the issue of whether the Eleventh Amendment permits a prisoner to secure money damages from a state for state actions that violate the ADA but not the Constitution. In addition, the Supreme Court decided *Arbaugh v. Y. & H Corp.*,[6] a case under Title VII of the Civil Rights Act of 1964, which has implications for the ADA's prohibition of discrimination where employers employ 15 or more employees.

On December 7, 2007, the Supreme Court granted certiorari in *Huber v. Wal-Mart Stores,*[7] to determine whether an individual with a disability who cannot perform her current job must be reassigned to a vacant, equivalent position without competing with other workers. However, the Court dismissed the petition since the case was settled prior to oral argument. Currently, there is a split in the circuits on this accommodation issue, and in light of the Court's dismissal of the case, there will continue to be divergent views.[8]

Before examining the provisions of the ADA and these cases, it is important to briefly note the ADA's historical antecedents. A federal statutory provision which existed prior to the ADA, Section 504 of the Rehabilitation Act of 1973, prohibits discrimination against an otherwise qualified individual with a disability, solely on the basis of the disability, in any program or activity that receives federal financial assistance, the executive agencies or the U.S. Postal Service.[9] Many of the concepts used in the ADA originated in Section 504 and its interpretations; however, there is one major difference. While Section 504's prohibition against discrimination is tied to the receipt of federal financial assistance, the ADA also covers entities not receiving such funds. In addition, the federal executive agencies and the U.S. Postal Service are covered under Section 504, not the ADA. The ADA contains a specific provision stating that except as otherwise provided in the act, nothing in the act shall be construed to apply a lesser standard than the standards applied under Title V of the Rehabilitation Act (which includes Section 504) or the regulations issued by federal agencies pursuant to such Title.[10]

The ADA is a civil rights statute; it does not provide grant funds to help entities comply with its requirements. It does include a section on technical assistance which authorizes grants and awards for the purpose of technical assistance such as the dissemination of information about rights under the ADA and techniques for effective compliance.[11] However, there are tax code provisions which may assist certain businesses or individuals.[12]

DEFINITION OF DISABILITY

Statutory Language

Definition Language

The definitions in the ADA, particularly the definition of "disability," are the starting point for an analysis of rights provided by the law.[13] The term "disability," with respect to an individual, is defined as "(A) a physical or mental impairment that substantially limits one or more of the major life activities of such individual; (B) a record of such an impairment; or (C) being regarded as having such an impairment (as described in paragraph (3))."[14] The definition of disability was the subject of numerous cases brought under the ADA including major Supreme Court decisions which generally interpreted the definition narrowly. Due to these interpretations, Congress enacted the ADA Amendments Act, which kept essentially the same statutory language but contains new rules of construction regarding the definition of disability. These rules of construction provide that

- the definition of disability shall be construed in favor of broad coverage to the maximum extent permitted by the terms of the act;
- the term "substantially limits" shall be interpreted consistently with the findings and purposes of the ADA Amendments Act;
- an impairment that substantially limits one major life activity need not limit other major life activities to be considered a disability;
- an impairment that is episodic or in remission is a disability if it would have substantially limited a major life activity when active;

- the determination of whether an impairment substantially limits a major life activity shall be made without regard to the ameliorative effects of mitigating measures, except that the ameliorative effects of ordinary eyeglasses or contact lenses shall be considered.[15]

The final EEOC regulations track the statutory definition but also provide some clarifying interpretations. For example, the operation of major bodily functions is included in the definition of major life activities. In addition, although the EEOC emphasizes the ADAAA's requirement for an individualized assessment, the regulations list some impairments that will almost always be determined to be a disability. These include deafness, blindness, an intellectual disability, missing limbs or mobility impairments requiring the use of a wheelchair, autism, cancer, cerebral palsy, diabetes, epilepsy, HIV infection, multiple sclerosis, muscular dystrophy, major depressive disorder, bipolar disorder, post-traumatic stress disorder, obsessive compulsive disorder, and schizophrenia.[16]

Statement of Findings and Purposes Regarding the Definition

The findings of the ADA Amendments Act include statements indicating that the Supreme Court decisions in *Sutton v. United Air Lines, Inc.*,[17] and *Toyota Motor Manufacturing v. Williams*[18] as well as lower court cases have narrowed and limited the ADA from what was intended by Congress. The codified findings in the original ADA are amended to delete the finding that "43,000,000 Americans have one or more physical or mental disabilities...." This finding was used in *Sutton* to support limiting the reach of the definition of disability. P.L. 110-325 specifically states that the current EEOC regulations defining the term "substantially limits" as "significantly restricted" are "inconsistent with congressional intent, by expressing too high a standard." The EEOC has promulgated regulations under the ADA Amendments Act which change the definition of "substantially limits."[19]

The ADA Amendments Act states that the purposes of the legislation are to carry out the ADA's objectives of the elimination of discrimination and the provision of "'clear, strong, consistent, enforceable standards addressing discrimination' by reinstating a broad scope of protection available under the ADA." P.L. 110-325 rejected the Supreme Court's holdings that mitigating measures are to be used in making a determination of whether an impairment substantially limits a major life activity as well as holdings defining the "substantially limits" requirements. The substantially limits requirements of

Toyota as well as the former EEOC regulations defining substantially limits as "significantly restricted" are specifically rejected in the new law.

Major Life Activities

The ADA Amendments Act specifically lists examples of major life activities including caring for oneself, performing manual tasks, seeing, hearing, eating, sleeping, walking, standing, lifting, bending, speaking, breathing, learning, reading, concentrating, thinking, communicating, and working. The act also states that a major life activity includes the operation of a major bodily function. The House Judiciary Committee report indicates that "this clarification was needed to ensure that the impact of an impairment on the operation of major bodily functions is not overlooked or wrongly dismissed as falling outside the definition of 'major life activities' under the ADA."[20] There had been judicial decisions which found that certain bodily functions had not been covered by the definition of disability. For example, in *Furnish v. SVI Sys., Inc.,*[21] the Seventh Circuit held that an individual with cirrhosis of the liver due to infection with Hepatitis B was not an individual with a disability because liver function was not "integral to one's daily existence."

Regarded as Having a Disability

The third prong of the definition of disability covers individuals who are "regarded as having such an impairment (as described in paragraph (3))." Paragraph 3 states that "[a]n individual meets the requirement of 'being regarded as having such an impairment' if the individual establishes that he or she has been subjected to an action prohibited under this Act because of an actual or perceived physical or mental impairment whether or not the impairment limits or is perceived to limit a major life activity." However, impairments that are transitory and minor are specifically excluded from the regarded prong. A transitory impairment is one with an actual or expected duration of six months or less. The ADA Amendments Act also provides in a rule of construction in Title V of the ADA that a covered entity under Title I,[22] a public entity under Title II, or a person who operates a place of public accommodation under Title III, need not provide a reasonable accommodation or a reasonable modification to policies, practices, or procedures to an individual who meets the definition of disability solely under the "regarded as" prong of the definition.

Regulatory Authority to Promulgate Regulations Regarding the Definition of Disability

The Supreme Court in *Sutton* questioned the authority of regulatory agencies to promulgate regulations for the definition of disability in the ADA. The definition of disability is contained in Section 3 of the ADA, and the ADA does not specifically give any agency the authority to interpret the definitions in Section 3, including the definition of disability. The Supreme Court declined to address this issue since, as both parties to *Sutton* accepted the regulation as valid, "we have no occasion to consider what deference they are due, if any." The ADA Amendments Act specifically grants regulatory authority and states that "[t]he authority to issue regulations granted to the Equal Employment Opportunity Commission, the Attorney General, and the Secretary of Transportation under this Act, includes the authority to issue regulations implementing the definitions contained in sections 3 and 4."

Title V Provisions on the Definition of Disability

The definition of "disability" was further elaborated in Title V of the ADA. Section 510 provides that the term "individual with a disability" in the ADA does not include an individual who is currently engaging in the illegal use of drugs when the covered entity acts on the basis of such use.[23] An individual who has been rehabilitated would be covered. However, the conference report language clarifies that the provision does not permit individuals to invoke coverage simply by showing they are participating in a drug rehabilitation program; they must refrain from using drugs.[24] The conference report also indicates that the limitation in coverage is not intended to be narrowly construed to only persons who use drugs "on the day of, or within a matter of weeks before, the action in question."[25] The definitional section of the Rehabilitation Act was also amended to create uniformity with this definition.

Section 508 provides that an individual shall not be considered to have a disability solely because that individual is a transvestite.[26] Section 511 similarly provides that homosexuality and bisexuality are not disabilities under the act and that the term disability does not include transvestism, transsexualism, pedophilia, exhibitionism, voyeurism, gender identity disorders not resulting from physical impairments, or other sexual behavior disorders, compulsive gambling, kleptomania, or pyromania, or psychoactive substance use disorders resulting from current illegal use of drugs.[27]

Supreme Court Cases

The Supreme Court has decided several cases relating to the definition of disability. The first ADA case to address the definitional issue was *Bragdon v. Abbott*, a case involving a dentist who refused to treat an HIV infected individual outside of a hospital.[28] In *Bragdon,* the Court found that the plaintiff's asymptomatic HIV infection was a physical impairment impacting on the major life activity of reproduction thus rending HIV infection a disability under the ADA. The other decisions—*Sutton v. United Airlines,*[29] *Murphy v. United Parcel Service, Inc.,*[30] *Albertsons Inc. v. Kirkingburg,*[31] and *Toyota Motor Manufacturing v. Williams*[32]—all involved issues which Congress later addressed in the ADA Amendments Act. Thus, although these decisions are of historical interest, especially regarding the impetus for the enactment of the ADA Amendments Act, they can no longer be assumed to be valid precedent and therefore will only be briefly discussed here.

Bragdon v. Abbott

The Supreme Court in *Bragdon v. Abbott* addressed the ADA definition of individual with a disability and held that the respondent's asymptomatic HIV infection was a physical impairment impacting on the major life activity of reproduction thus rendering the HIV infection a disability under the ADA.[33] In 1994, Dr. Bragdon performed a dental examination on Ms. Abbott and discovered a cavity. Ms. Abbott had indicated in her registration form that she was HIV positive but at that time she was asymptomatic. Dr. Bragdon told her that he would not fill her cavity in his office but would treat her only in a hospital setting. Ms. Abbott filed an ADA complaint and prevailed at the district court, courts of appeals and the Supreme Court on the issue of whether she was an individual with a disability but the case was remanded for further consideration regarding the issue of direct threat.

In arriving at its holding, Justice Kennedy, writing for the majority, first looked to whether Ms. Abbott's HIV infection was a physical impairment. Noting the immediacy with which the HIV virus begins to damage an individual's white blood cells, the Court found that asymptomatic HIV infection was a physical impairment. Second, the Court examined whether this physical impairment affected a major life activity and concluded that the HIV infection placed a substantial limitation on her ability to reproduce and to bear children and that reproduction was a major life activity. Finally, the Court examined whether the physical impairment was a substantial limitation on the major life activity of reproduction. After evaluating the medical evidence, the Court concluded that Ms. Abbott's ability to reproduce was substantially limited in two ways: (1) an attempt to conceive would impose a significant risk on Ms. Abbott's partner, and (2) an HIV infected woman risks infecting her child during gestation and childbirth.[34]

Sutton v. United Airlines, Murphy v. United Parcel Service, and Albertsons, Inc. v Kirkingburg

Three Supreme Court decisions in 1999 addressed the definition of disability and specifically discussed the concept of mitigating measures. *Sutton v. United Air Lines* involved sisters who were rejected from employment as pilots with United Air Lines because they wore eyeglasses. The Supreme Court in *Sutton* examined the definition of disability used in the original ADA and found that the determination of whether an individual has a disability should be made with reference to measures that mitigate the individual's impairment. The *Sutton* Court stated: "'a disability' exists only where an impairment 'substantially limits' a major life activity, not where it 'might,' 'could,' or 'would' be substantially limiting if mitigating measures were not taken." The Court also emphasized that the statement of findings in the ADA that some 43,000,000 Americans have one or more physical or mental disability "requires the conclusion that Congress did not intend to bring under the statute's protection all those whose uncorrected conditions amount to disabilities."

Similarly, in *Murphy v. United Parcel Service, Inc.*, the Court held that the fact that an individual with high blood pressure was unable to meet the Department of Transportation (DOT) safety standards was not sufficient to create an issue of fact regarding whether an individual is regarded as unable to utilize a class of jobs. The Court in *Murphy* found that an employee is regarded as having a disability if the covered entity mistakenly believes that the employee's actual, nonlimiting impairment substantially limits one or more major life activities. And in the last of this trilogy of 1999 cases, the Court in *Albertsons v. Kirkingburg* held that a trucker with monocular vision who was able to compensate for this impairment was not a person with a disability.

Toyota Motor Manufacturing of Kentucky v. Williams

In the 2002 case of *Toyota Motor Manufacturing v. Williams,* the meaning of "substantially limits" was examined, and Justice O'Connor, writing for the unanimous Court, determined that the word substantial "clearly precluded impairments that interfere in only a minor way with the performance of manual tasks." The Court also found that the term "major life activity" "refers to those activities that are of central importance to daily life." Finding that these terms are to be "interpreted strictly," the Court held that "to be substantially limited in performing manual tasks, an individual must have an impairment that prevents or severely restricts the individual from doing activities that are of central importance to most people's daily lives."

APPLICATION OF THE ELEVENTH AMENDMENT TO THE ADA

The Eleventh Amendment states: "The Judicial power of the United States shall not be construed to extend to any suit in law or equity, commenced or prosecuted against one of the United States by Citizens of another State, or by Citizens or Subjects of any Foreign State." The Supreme Court has found that the Eleventh Amendment cannot be abrogated by the use of Article I powers but that Section 5 of the Fourteenth Amendment can be used for abrogation in certain circumstances. Section 5 of the Fourteenth Amendment states: "The Congress shall have the power to enforce, by appropriate legislation, the provisions of this article."

The circumstances where Section 5 of the Fourteenth Amendment can be used to abrogate the Eleventh Amendment were discussed in the Supreme Court decisions in *College Savings Bank v. Florida Prepaid Postsecondary Educ. Expense Board,*[35] *Florida Prepaid Postsecondary Educ. Expense Board v. College Savings Bank,*[36] and *Kimel v. Florida Board of Regents.*[37] They reiterated the principle that the Congress may abrogate state immunity from suit under the Fourteenth Amendment and found that there were three conditions necessary for successful abrogation.

- Congressional power is limited to the enactment of "appropriate" legislation to enforce the substantive provisions of the Fourteenth Amendment.
- The legislation must be remedial in nature.
- There must be a "congruence and proportionality" between the injury to be prevented and the means adopted to that end.

The ADA uses both the Fourteenth Amendment and the Commerce Clause of the Constitution as its constitutional basis.[38] It also specifically abrogates state immunity under the Eleventh Amendment.[39] The ADA, then, is clear regarding its attempt to abrogate state immunity; the issue is whether the other elements of a successful abrogation are present. The Supreme Court in *Garrett v. University of Alabama* found that they were not with regard to Title I while in *Tennessee v. Lane* the Court upheld Title II as it applies to the access to courts.[40] Most recently, the Supreme Court in *United States v. Georgia,*[41] held that Title II of the ADA created a private cause of action for damages against the states for conduct that actually violates the Fourteenth Amendment. However, the Court did not reach the issue of whether the Eleventh Amendment permits a prisoner to secure money damages from a state for state actions that violate the ADA but not the Constitution.

EMPLOYMENT

General Requirements

Statutory and Regulatory Requirements

Title I of the ADA, as amended by the ADA Amendments Act of 2008, provides that no covered entity shall discriminate against a qualified individual on the basis of disability in regard to job application procedures, the hiring, advancement, or discharge of employees, employee compensation, job training, and other terms, conditions, and privileges of employment.[42] The term *employer* is defined as a person engaged in an industry affecting commerce who has 15 or more employees.[43] Therefore, the employment section of the ADA, unlike the section on public accommodations, which will be discussed subsequently, is limited in scope to employers with 15 or more employees. This parallels the coverage provided in the Civil Rights Act of 1964. As noted previously, the Supreme Court, in *Arbaugh v. Y. & H. Corp.*,[44] held that the 15-employee limitation in Title VII of the Civil Rights Act[45] was not jurisdictional, but rather was related to the substantive adequacy of a claim. Thus, if the defense that the employer employs fewer than 15 employees is not raised in a timely manner, a court is not obligated to dismiss the case. Because the ADA's 15-employee limitation language parallels that of Title VII, it is likely that a court would interpret the ADA's requirement in the same manner.

The term *employee* with respect to employment in a foreign country includes an individual who is a citizen of the United States; however, it is not unlawful for a covered entity to take action that constitutes discrimination with respect to an employee in a workplace in a foreign country if compliance would cause the covered entity to violate the law of the foreign country.[46]

If the issue raised under the ADA is employment related, and the threshold issues of meeting the definition of an individual with a disability and involving an employer employing more than 15 individuals are met, the next step is to determine whether the individual is a qualified individual with a disability who, with or without reasonable accommodation, can perform the essential functions of the job.

Title I defines a "qualified individual with a disability." Such an individual is "an individual with a disability who, with or without reasonable accommodation, can perform the essential functions of the employment position that such person holds or desires."[47] The ADA incorporates many of the concepts set forth in the regulations promulgated pursuant to Section 504, including the requirement to provide reasonable accommodation unless the accommodation would pose an undue hardship on the operation of the business.[48]

"Reasonable accommodation" is defined in the ADA as including making existing facilities readily accessible to and usable by individuals with disabilities, and job restructuring, part-time or modified work schedules, reassignment to a vacant position, acquisition or modification of equipment or devices, adjustment of examinations or training materials or policies, provision of qualified readers or interpreters or other similar accommodations.[49] "Undue hardship" is defined as "an action requiring significant difficulty or expense."[50] Factors to be considered in determining whether an action would create an undue hardship include the nature and cost of the accommodation, the overall financial resources of the facility, the overall financial resources of the covered entity, and the type of operation or operations of the covered entity.

Reasonable accommodation and the related concept of undue hardship are significant concepts under the ADA and are one of the major ways in which the ADA is distinguishable from Title VII jurisprudence. The statutory language paraphrased above provides some guidance for employers but the details of the requirements have been the subject of numerous judicial decisions. In addition, the EEOC issued detailed enforcement guidance on these concepts on March 1, 1999,[51] which was amended on October 17, 2002, to reflect the Supreme Court's decision in *U.S. Airways v. Barnett.*[52] Although much of the guidance reiterates long-standing EEOC interpretations in a question and answer format, the EEOC also took issue with some judicial interpretations.[53] Notably the EEOC stated that

- an employee who is granted leave as a reasonable accommodation is entitled to return to his or her same position, unless this imposes an undue hardship; and
- an employer is limited in the ability to question the employee's documentation of a disability ("An employer cannot ask for documentation when: (1) both the disability and the need for reasonable accommodation are obvious, or (2) the individual has already provided the employer with sufficient information to substantiate that s/he has an ADA disability and needs the reasonable accommodation requested.").

Issues regarding the amount of money that must be spent on reasonable accommodations have also arisen. The EEOC regulations[54] and guidance provide that an employer does not have to provide a reasonable accommodation that would cause an "undue hardship" to the employer.[55] However, the Seventh Circuit in *Vande Zande v. State of Wisconsin Department of Administration*[56] found that the cost of the accommodation cannot be disproportionate to the benefit. "Even if an employer is so large or wealthy—or, like the principal defendant in this case, is a state, which can raise taxes in order to finance any accommodations that it must make to disabled employees—that it may not be able to plead 'undue hardship', it would not be required to expend enormous sums in order to bring about a trivial improvement in the life of a disabled employee."[57]

Clackamas Gastroenterology Associates P.C. v. Wells

The Supreme Court examined the definition of the term "employee" under the ADA in *Clackamas Gastroenterology Associates P.C. v. Wells.*[58] In *Clackamas,* the Court held in a 7-2 decision written by Justice Stevens, that the EEOC's guidelines concerning whether a shareholder-director is an employee were the correct standard to use. Since the evidence was not clear, the case was remanded for further proceedings. Clackamas Gastroenterology Associates is a medical clinic in Oregon that employed Ms. Wells as a bookkeeper from 1986-1997. After her termination from employment, Ms. Wells brought an action alleging unlawful discrimination on the basis of discrimination under Title I of the ADA. The clinic denied that it was covered by the ADA since it argued that it did not have 15 or more employees for the 20 weeks per year required by the statute. The determination of coverage was dependent on whether the four physician-shareholders who owned the professional corporation were counted as employees.

The Court first looked to the definition of employee in the ADA which states that an employee is "an individual employed by an employer."[59] This definition was described as one which is "completely circular and explains nothing." The majority then looked to common law, specifically the common law element of control. This is the position advocated by the EEOC. The EEOC has issued guidelines which list six factors to be considered in determining whether the individual acts independently and participates in managing the organization or whether the individual is subject to the organization's control and therefore an employee. These six factors are:

> Whether the organization can hire or fire the individual or set the rules and regulations of the individual's work; Whether and, if so, to what extent the organization supervises the individual's work; Whether the individual reports to someone higher in the organization; Whether and, if so, to what extent the individual is able to influence the organization; Whether the parties intended that the individual be an employee, as expressed in written agreements or contracts; and Whether the individual shares in the profits, losses, and liabilities of the organization.[60]

Justice Stevens, writing for the majority, found that some of the district court's findings of fact, when considered in light of the EEOC's standard, appeared to favor the conclusion that the four physicians were not employees of the clinic. However, since there was some evidence that might support the opposite conclusion, the Court remanded the case for further proceedings.

Justice Ginsburg, joined by Justice Breyer, dissented from the majority's opinion. The dissenters argued that the Court's opinion used only one of the common-law aspects of a master-servant relationship. In addition, Justice Ginsburg noted that the physician-shareholders argued they were employees for the purposes of other statutes, notably the Employee Retirement Income Security Act of 1974 (ERISA) and stated "I see no reason to allow the doctors to escape from their choice of corporate form when the question becomes whether they are employees for the purposes of federal antidiscrimination statutes."

Other Supreme Court Employment Cases

Many of the Supreme Court decisions have involved employment situations although a number of these cases did not reach past the threshold issue of whether the individual alleging employment discrimination was an individual with a disability. There are still several significant employment issues, such as reasonable accommodations, which have not been dealt with by the Court. In addition, the landmark decision of *University of Alabama v. Garrett* on the application of the Eleventh Amendment arose in the employment context.

Receipt of SSI Benefits

The relationship between the receipt of SSDI benefits and the ability of an individual to pursue an ADA employment claim was the issue in *Cleveland v. Policy Management Systems Corp, supra*. The Supreme Court unanimously held that pursuit and receipt of SSDI benefits does not automatically stop a recipient from pursuing an ADA claim or even create a strong presumption against success under the ADA. Observing that the Social Security Act and the ADA both help individuals with disabilities but in different ways, the Court found that "despite the appearance of conflict that arises from the language of the two statutes, the two claims do not inherently conflict to the point where courts should apply a special negative presumption like the one applied by the Court of Appeals here." The fact that the ADA defines a qualified individual as one who can perform the essential functions of the job with or without reasonable accommodation was seen as a key distinction between the ADA and the Social Security Act. In addition, the Court observed that SSDI benefits are sometimes granted to individuals who are working.

The Seventh Circuit, in *Johnson v. ExxonmobilCorp.*,[61] applied the Supreme Court's analysis in *Cleveland* and distinguished the factual situations. In *Cleveland* the plaintiff had argued that she had made consistent statements in her ADA claim and in the SSDI application; however, in *Johnson* the Seventh Circuit found that the plaintiff had merely argued that "he was mistaken in his SSDI application." The court of appeals concluded that "*Cleveland* does not stand for the proposition that defendants should be allowed to explain why they gave false statements on their SSDI applications, which is essentially what Johnson seeks to do here."[62]

"Qualified" Individual with a Disability

In *Albertsons, Inc. v. Kirkingburg,*[63] the Supreme Court held that an employer need not adopt an experimental vision waiver program. Title I of the ADA prohibits discrimination in employment against a "qualified" individual with a disability. In finding that the plaintiff's inability to comply with the general regulatory vision requirements rendered him unqualified, the Court framed the question in the following manner. “Is it reasonable ... to read the ADA as requiring an employer like Albertsons to shoulder the general statutory burden to justify a job qualification that would tend to exclude the disabled, whenever the employer chooses to abide by the otherwise clearly applicable, unamended substantive regulatory standard despite the Government’s willingness to waive it experimentally and without any finding of its being inappropriate?” Answering this question in the negative, the Court observed that employers should not be required to “reinvent the Government’s own wheel” and stated that “it is simply not credible that Congress enacted the ADA (before there was any waiver program) with the understanding that employers choosing to respect the Government’s sole substantive visual acuity regulation in the face of an experimental waiver might be burdened with an obligation to defend the regulation’s application according to its own terms.”

In *Chevron U.S.A. Inc., v. Echazabal,*[64] the Supreme Court held unanimously that the ADA does not require an employer to hire an individual with a disability if the job in question would endanger the individual’s health. The ADA’s statutory language provides for a defense to an allegation of discrimination that a qualification standard is “job related and consistent with business necessity.”[65] The act also allows an employer to impose as a qualification standard that the individual shall not pose a direct threat to the health or safety of other individuals in the workplace[66] but does not discuss a threat to the individual’s health or safety. The Ninth Circuit in *Echazabal* had determined that an employer violated the ADA by refusing to hire an applicant with a serious liver condition whose illness would be aggravated through exposure to the chemicals in the workplace.[67] The Supreme Court rejected the Ninth Circuit decision and upheld a regulation by the EEOC that allows an employer to assert a direct threat defense to an allegation of employment discrimination where the threat is posed only to the health or safety of the individual making the allegation.[68] Justice Souter found that the EEOC regulations were not the kind of workplace paternalism that the ADA seeks to outlaw. “The EEOC was certainly acting within the reasonable zone when it saw a difference between rejecting workplace paternalism and ignoring specific and documented risks to the employee himself, even if the employee would take his chances for the sake of getting a job.” The Court emphasized that a direct threat defense must be based on medical judgment that uses the most current medical knowledge.

The Supreme Court had examined an analogous issue in *UAW v. Johnson Controls, Inc.,*[69] which held that under the Civil Rights Act of 1964 employers could not enforce "fetal protection" policies that kept women, whether pregnant or with the potential to become pregnant, from jobs that might endanger a developing fetus. Although this case was raised by the plaintiff, the Supreme Court distinguished the decision there from that in *Echazabal*. The *Johnson Controls* decision was described as "concerned with paternalistic judgments based on the broad category of gender, while the EEOC has required that judgments based on the direct threat provision be made on the basis of individualized risk assessments."

Collective Bargaining Agreements

The interplay between rights under the ADA and collective bargaining agreements was the subject of the Supreme Court's decision in *Wright v. Universal Maritime Service Corp., supra.* The Court held there that the general arbitration clause in a collective bargaining agreement does not require a plaintiff to use the arbitration procedure for an alleged violation of the ADA. However, the Court's decision was limited since the Court did not find it necessary to reach the issue of the validity of a union-negotiated waiver. In other words, the Court found that a general arbitration agreement in a collective bargaining agreement is not sufficient to waive rights under civil rights statutes but situations where there is a specific waiver of ADA rights were not addressed.[70]

Reasonable Accommodations and Seniority Systems

The Supreme Court in *U.S. Airways v. Barnett*[71] held that an employer's showing that a requested accommodation by an employee with a disability conflicts with the rules of a seniority system is ordinarily sufficient to establish that the requested accommodation is not "reasonable" within the meaning of the ADA. The Court, in a majority opinion by Justice Breyer, observed that a seniority system, "provides important employee benefits by creating, and fulfilling, employee expectations of fair, uniform treatment" and that to require a "typical employer to show more than the existence of a seniority system might undermine the employees' expectations of consistent, uniform treatment." Thus, in most ADA cases, the existence of a seniority system would entitle an employer to summary judgment in its favor. The Court found no language in the ADA which would change this presumption if the seniority system was imposed by management and not by collective bargaining. However, Justice Breyer found that there were some exceptions to this rule for "special circumstances" and gave as examples situations where (1) the employer "fairly frequently" changes the seniority system unilaterally, and thereby diminishes employee expectations to the point where one more departure would "not likely make a difference" or (2) the seniority system contains so many exceptions that one more exception is unlikely to matter.

Although the majority in *Barnett* garnered five votes, the Court's views were splintered. There were strong dissents and two concurring opinions. In her concurrence, Justice O'Connor stated that she would prefer to say that the effect of a seniority system on the ADA depends on whether the seniority system is legally enforceable but that since the result would be the same in most cases as under the majority's reasoning, she joined with the majority to prevent a stalemate. The dissents took vigorous exception to the majority's decision with Justice Scalia, joined by Justice Thomas, arguing that the ADA does not permit any seniority system to be overridden. The dissent by Justice Souter, joined by Justice Ginsberg, argued that nothing in the ADA insulated seniority rules from a reasonable accommodation requirement and that the legislative history of the ADA clearly indicated congressional intent that seniority systems be a factor in reasonable accommodations determinations but not the major factor.

Rehiring of Individual Who Has been Terminated for Illegal Drug Use

In *Raytheon Co. v. Hernandez*,[72] the Supreme Court was presented with the issue of whether the ADA confers preferential rehiring rights on employees who have been lawfully terminated for misconduct, in this case illegal drug use. However, the Court, in an opinion by Justice Thomas, did not reach this issue, finding that the Ninth Circuit had improperly applied a disparate impact analysis in a disparate treatment case and remanding the case. The Court observed that it "has consistently recognized a distinction between claims of discrimination based on disparate treatment and claims of discrimination based on disparate impact." Disparate treatment was described as when an employer intentionally treats some people less favorably than others because of a protected characteristic such as race and liability depends on whether the protected trait actually motivated the employer's decision. Disparate impact, in contrast, involves practices that are facially neutral but in fact impact a protected group more harshly and cannot be justified by business necessity. Disparate impact cases do not require evidence of an employer's subjective intent.[73]

Employment Inquiries Relating to a Disability

Before an offer of employment is made, an employer may not ask a disability related question or require a medical examination.[74] The EEOC in its guidance on this issue stated that the rationale for this exclusion was to isolate an employer's consideration of an applicant's non-medical qualifications from any consideration of the applicant's medical condition.[75] Once an offer is made, disability related questions and medical examinations are permitted as long as all individuals who have been offered a job in that category are asked the same questions and given the same examinations.[76] It is not always clear exactly what is a medical test. In *Karraker v. Rent- a-Center, Inc.,*[77] the Seventh Circuit examined the issue of whether an employer's use of the Minnesota Multiphasic Personality Inventory (MMPI) in order to obtain a promotion violated the ADA. The MMPI contains questions such as "I commonly hear voices without knowing where they are coming from" and "I see things or animals or people around me that others do not see." The court found that, even though the test was not interpreted by a psychologist, the MMPI was a medical test since it was designed in part to reveal mental illness.

The events of September 11, 2001, raised questions concerning whether an employer may ask employees whether they will require assistance in the event of an evacuation because of a disability or medical condition. The EEOC issued a fact sheet stating that employers are allowed to ask employees to self-identify if they will require assistance because of a disability or medical conditions and providing details on how the employer may identify individuals who may require assistance.[78] Similarly, the 2009 H1N1 influenza pandemic also raised issues concerning inquiries relating to a disability, and the EEOC has issued guidance for employers.[79]

Defenses to a Charge of Discrimination

The ADA specifically lists defenses that may be applied to a charge of discrimination. If an employer can demonstrate that qualification standards, tests, or other selection criteria that may disqualify an individual with a disability are "job-related, … consistent with business necessity, and such performance cannot be accomplished by reasonable accommodation," the employer may not be liable under the ADA.[80] The ADA further states that such standards, tests, and criteria may not be used to disqualify an individual based on his or her uncorrected vision unless the requirement is job-related and consistent with business necessity.[81]

Employers may discriminate against an individual with a disability if he or she poses a direct threat to the health or safety of other individuals in the workplace.[82] The EEOC has indicated that the following factors should be considered when determining whether an individual poses a direct threat: the duration of the risk; the nature and severity of the potential harm; the likelihood that the potential harm will occur; and the imminence of the potential harm.[83]

The ADA includes two exceptions for religious organizations. First, religious entities may "[give] preference in employment to individuals of a particular religion to perform work connected with the carrying on by such [entity] of its activities."[84] Second, religious entities may require applicants and employees to conform to their religious tenets.[85] In addition to these statutory protections, the Supreme Court has affirmed additional constitutional protections available to religious employers. In *Hosanna-Tabor Evangelical Lutheran Church and School v. EEOC,* a teacher at a religious school challenged her termination under the ADA after the school fired her following her disability leave.[86] The Court recognized the constitutional ministerial exception to employment discrimination laws, explaining that religious institutions must be permitted to select employees who are responsible for carrying out the institution's mission.[87] Thus, the ministerial exception may be claimed by religious employers with respect to ministers and ministerial employees only. The ministerial exception prevents governmental interference in decisions regarding these employees in conformance with the constitutional requirements of the First Amendment.[88]

Finally, employers may avoid liability under the ADA for decisions that discriminate against individuals with an infectious or communicable disease if the disease may be transmitted through food handling and the job involves such duties.[89] To claim this defense, the disease must be listed by the Secretary of Health And Human Services as an infectious disease transmitted through food handling and must not be able to be eliminated by reasonable accommodation.[90]

Drugs, Alcohol, and Employer Conduct Rules

A controversial issue that arose during the enactment of the ADA regarding employment concerned the application of the act to drug addicts and alcoholics. The ADA provides that, with regard to employment, *current* illegal drug users are not considered to be qualified individuals with disabilities. However, former drug users and alcoholics would be covered by the act if they are able to perform the essential functions of the job. Exactly what is "current" use of illegal drugs has been the subject of some discussion. The EEOC has defined current to mean that the illegal drug use occurred "recently enough" to justify an employer's reasonable belief that drug use is an ongoing problem.[91] The courts that have examined this issue have generally found that to be covered by the ADA, the individual must be free of drugs for a considerable period of time, certainly longer than weeks.[92]

In the appendix to its regulations, EEOC further notes that "an employer, such as a law enforcement agency, may also be able to impose a qualification standard that excludes individuals with a history of illegal use of drugs if it can show that the standard is job-related and consistent with business necessity."[93] Title I of the ADA also provides that a covered entity may prohibit the illegal use of drugs and the use of alcohol in the workplace.[94] Similarly, employers may hold all employees, regardless of whether or not they have a disability, to the same performance and conduct standards.[95] However, if the misconduct results from a disability, the employer must be able to demonstrate that the rule is job-related and consistent with business necessity.[96]

Remedies

The remedies and procedures set forth in Sections 705, 706, 707, 709, and 710 of the Civil Rights Act of 1964,[97] are incorporated by reference. This provides for certain administrative enforcement as well as allowing for individual suits. The Civil Rights Act of 1991, P.L. 102-166, expanded the remedies of injunctive relief and back pay. A plaintiff who was the subject of unlawful intentional discrimination (as opposed to an employment practice that is discriminatory because of its disparate impact) may recover compensatory and punitive damages. In order to receive punitive damages, the plaintiff must show that there was a discriminatory practice engaged in with malice or with reckless indifference to the rights of the aggrieved individuals. The amount that can be awarded in punitive and compensatory damages is capped, with the amounts varying from $50,000 to $300,000 depending upon the size of the business.[98] Similarly, there is also a "good faith" exception to the award of damages with regard to reasonable accommodation.

The Lilly Ledbetter Fair Pay Act of 2009, P.L. 111-2, amends Title VII of the Civil Rights Act of 1964, the Age Discrimination in Employment Act, the Rehabilitation Act of 1973, and the Americans with Disabilities Act. Enacted in response to the Supreme Court's decision in *Ledbetter v. Goodyear Tire & Rubber Co.,*[99] the law states that an unlawful employment practice occurs, with respect to discrimination in compensation, when a discriminatory compensation decision or other practice is adopted, when an individual becomes subject to a discriminatory compensation decision or practice, or when an individual is affected by application of a discriminatory compensation decision or practice. Liability for these discriminatory practices may accrue and an individual may obtain back pay for up to two years preceding the filing of the charges.[100] P.L. 111-2 applies to Title I of the ADA which covers employment, and Section 503, 42 U.S.C. §12203, of the ADA, which prohibits retaliation and coercion.

It should also be noted that the Supreme Court addressed the issue of punitive damages in a Title VII sex discrimination case, *Kolstad v. American Dental Association.*[101] The Court held in *Kolstad* that plaintiffs are not required to prove egregious conduct to be awarded punitive damages; however, the effect of this holding is limited by the Court's determination that certain steps taken by an employer may immunize them from punitive damages. Since the ADA incorporates the Title VII provisions, the holding in *Kolstad* may be applicable to ADA employment cases as well.[102]

In *Equal Employment Opportunity Commission v. Wal-mart Stores, Inc.,*[103] the Tenth Circuit applied *Kolstad* and affirmed an award of punitive damages under the ADA. This case involved a hearing impaired employee of Wal-mart who sometimes required the assistance of an interpreter. After being employed for about two years in the receiving department, the employee was required to attend a training session but left when the video tape shown was not close captioned and no interpreter was provided. After refusing to attend in the absence of an interpreter, the employee was transferred to the maintenance department to perform janitorial duties. When he questioned the transfer and asked for an interpreter, he was again denied. After threatening to file a complaint with the EEOC, the employee was suspended and later terminated from employment. He then sued and won compensatory damages and $75,000 in punitive damages. On appeal, the Tenth Circuit examined the reasoning in *Kolstad* and concluded that the record in *Wal-mart* "is sufficient to resolve the questions of intent and agency laid out in *Kolstad.*" With regard to intent, the court reiterated the facts and further noted that the store manager, who ultimately approved the employee's suspension, had testified that he was familiar with the ADA and its provisions regarding accommodation, discrimination and retaliation. This was seen as sufficient for a reasonable jury to conclude that Wal-mart intentionally discriminated. Wal-mart had also made an agency argument, stating that liability for punitive damages was improper because the employees who discriminated against the employee did not occupy positions of managerial control. Looking again to the reasoning in *Kolstad*, the Tenth Circuit noted that the Wal-mart employees had authority regarding hiring and firing decisions and observed that such authority is an indicium of supervisory or managerial capacity.

PUBLIC SERVICES

General Requirements

Title II of the ADA provides that no qualified individual with a disability shall be excluded from participation in or be denied the benefits of the services, programs, or activities of a public entity or be subjected to discrimination by any such entity.[104] "Public entity" is defined as state and local governments, any department or other instrumentality of a state or local government and certain transportation authorities. The ADA does not apply to the executive branch of the federal government; the executive branch and the U.S. Postal Service are covered by Section 504 of the Rehabilitation Act of 1973.[105]

The Department of Justice (DOJ) promulgated regulations for Title II which were amended as published in the *Federal Register* on September 15, 2010. The regulations contain a specific section on program accessibility. Each service, program, or activity conducted by a public entity, when viewed in its entirety, must be readily accessible to and usable by individuals with disabilities. However, a public entity is not required to make each of its existing facilities accessible.[106] Program accessibility is limited in certain situations involving historic preservation. In addition, in meeting the program accessibility requirement, a public entity is not required to take any action that would result in a fundamental alteration in the nature of its service, program, or activity or in undue financial and administrative burdens.[107] The amended Title II regulations adopt accessibility standards consistent with the new minimum guidelines and requirements issued by the Architectural and Transportation Barriers Compliance Board (Access Board). In order to provide "an important measure of clarity and certainty for public entities,"[108] DOJ's amended title II regulations add an "element by element safe harbor" provision where elements in covered facilities that were built or altered in accordance with the previous 1991 accessibility standards would not be required to be brought into compliance with the new standards until the elements were subject to a planned alteration. In addition, the amended regulations include more detailed standards for service animals,[109] power-driven mobility devices, ticketing, and effective communication.[110] The amended regulations took effect March 15, 2011, but compliance with the 2010 standards for accessible design is not required until March 15, 2012.

Title II of the ADA would also apply to state and local government emergency preparedness and response programs. The Department of Justice has issued an ADA guide for local governments, noting that "one of the most important roles of local government is to protect their citizenry from harm, including helping people prepare for and respond to emergencies. Making local government emergency preparedness and response programs accessible to people with disabilities is critical part of this responsibility. Making these programs accessible is also required by the ADA."[111]

Supreme Court Cases

Although Title II has not been the subject of as much litigation as Title I, several of the ADA cases to reach the Supreme Court have involved Title II. The most significant of these to date is *Tennessee v. Lane.*[112] In *Lane*, the Supreme Court held that Title II of the ADA, as it applies to the fundamental right of access to the courts, constitutes a valid exercise of congressional authority under Section 5 of the Fourteenth Amendment. In addition, the Supreme Court in *United States v. Georgia.,*[113] held that Title II of the ADA created a private cause of action for damages against the states for conduct that actually violates the Fourteenth Amendment.

In the first ADA case to reach the Supreme Court, *Pennsylvania Department of Corrections v. Yeskey, supra,* the Court found in a unanimous decision that state prisons "fall squarely within the statutory definition of 'public entity'" for Title II. *Yeskey* involved a prisoner who was sentenced to 18 to 36 months in a Pennsylvania correctional facility but was recommended for placement in a motivational boot camp for first time offenders. If the boot camp was successfully completed, the prisoner would have been eligible for parole in six months. The prisoner was denied admission to the program due to his medical history of hypertension and sued under the ADA. The state argued that state prisoners were not covered under the ADA since such coverage would "alter the usual constitutional balance between the States and the Federal Government." The Supreme Court rejected this argument, observing that "the ADA plainly covers state institutions *without* any exception that could cast the coverage of prisons into doubt." The Court noted that prisoners receive many services, including medical services, educational and vocational programs and recreational activities so that the ADA language applying the "benefits of the services, programs, or activities of a public entity" is applicable to state prisons.[114] However, the Court in *Yeskey* did not address the constitutional issues.

In *Olmstead v. Georgia, supra,* the Supreme Court examined issues raised by state mental health institutions and held that Title II of the ADA requires states to place individuals with mental disabilities in community settings rather than institutions when the State's treatment professionals have determined that community placement is appropriate, community placement is not opposed by the individual with a disability, and the placement can be reasonably accommodated.[115] "Unjustified isolation ... is properly regarded as discrimination based on disability." The *Olmstead* case had been closely watched by both disability groups and state governments. Although disability groups have applauded the holding that undue institutionalization qualifies as discrimination by reason of disability, the Supreme Court did place certain limitations on this right. In addition to the agreement of the individual affected, the Court also dealt with the issue of what is a reasonable modification of an existing program and stated: "Sensibly construed, the fundamental-alteration component of the reasonable-modifications regulation would allow the State to show that, in the allocation of available resources, immediate relief for the plaintiffs would be inequitable, given the responsibility the State has undertaken for the care and treatment of a large and diverse population of persons with mental disabilities." This examination of what constitutes a reasonable modification may have implications for the interpretation of similar concepts in the employment and public accommodations Titles of the ADA.[116]

Other Title II Cases

Courts have examined various other issues regarding compliance with Title II. For example, in *Crowder v. Kitagawa*, a Hawaii regulation requiring the quarantine of all dogs, including guide dogs for visually impaired individuals, was found to violate Title II.[117] Other Title II cases have involved whether curb ramps are required,[118] the application of Title II to a city ordinance allowing open burning,[119] and the application of the ADA to a city's zoning ordinances.[120]

Transportation Provisions

Title II also provides specific requirements for public transportation by intercity and commuter rail and for public transportation other than by aircraft or certain rail operations.[121] All new vehicles purchased or leased by a public entity that operates a fixed route system must be accessible, and good faith efforts must be demonstrated with regard to the purchase or lease of accessible use vehicles. Retrofitting of existing buses is not required. Paratransit services must be provided by a public entity that operates a fixed route service, other than one providing solely commuter bus service.[122] Rail systems must have at least one car per train that is accessible to individuals with disabilities.[123]

Draft guidelines have been published by the Architectural and Transportation Barriers Compliance Board (Access Board) regarding the accessibility of public rights-of-way.[124] The purpose of the draft guidelines is to gather additional information for the regulatory assessment and the preparation of technical assistance materials to accompany a future rule. The Board will issue a notice of proposed rulemaking at a future date and will solicit comments at that time, prior to issuing a final rule.

Remedies

The enforcement remedies of Section 505 of the Rehabilitation Act of 1973, 29 U.S.C. §794a, are incorporated by reference.[125] These remedies are similar to those of Title VI of the Civil Rights Act of 1964, and include damages and injunctive relief. The Attorney General has promulgated regulations relating to subpart A of the Title,[126] and the Secretary of Transportation has issued regulations regarding transportation.[127]

Barnes v. Gorman

The Supreme Court in *Barnes v. Gorman*[128] held in a unanimous decision that punitive damages may not be awarded under Section 202[129] of the ADA and Section 504 of the Rehabilitation Act of 1973.[130] Jeffrey Gorman uses a wheelchair and lacks voluntary control over his lower torso which necessitates the use of a catheter attached to a urine bag. He was arrested in 1992 after fighting with a bouncer at a nightclub and during his transport to the police station suffered significant injuries due to the manner in which he was transported. He sued the Kansas City police and was awarded over $1 million in compensatory damages and $1.2 million in punitive damages. The Eighth Circuit court of appeals upheld the award of punitive damages but the Supreme Court reversed. Although the Court was unanimous in the result, there were two concurring opinions and the concurring opinion by Justice Stevens, joined by Justices Ginsburg and Breyer, disagreed with the reasoning used in Justice Scalia's opinion for the Court.

Justice Scalia observed that the remedies for violations of both Section 202 of the ADA and Section 504 of the Rehabilitation Act are "coextensive with the remedies available in a private cause of action brought under Title VI of the Civil Rights Act of 1964."[131] Neither Section 504 nor Title II of the ADA specifically mention punitive damages, rather they reference the remedies of Title VI of the Civil Rights Act. Title VI is based on the congressional power under the Spending Clause[132] to place conditions on grants. Justice Scalia noted that Spending Clause legislation is "much in the nature of a contract" and, in order to be a legitimate use of this power, the recipient must voluntarily and knowingly accept the terms of the "contract." "If Congress intends to impose a condition on the grant of federal moneys, it must do so unambiguously."[133] This contract law analogy was also found to be applicable to determining the scope of the damages remedies and, since punitive damages are generally not found to be available for a breach of contract, Justice Scalia found that they were not available under Title VI, Section 504 or the ADA.

PUBLIC ACCOMMODATIONS

General Requirements

Title III provides that no individual shall be discriminated against on the basis of disability in the full and equal enjoyment of the goods, services, facilities, privileges, advantages, or accommodations of any place of public accommodation by any person who owns, leases (or leases to), or operates a place of public accommodation.[134] Entities that are covered by the term "public accommodation" are listed, and include, among others, hotels, restaurants, theaters, auditoriums, laundromats, museums, parks, zoos, private schools, day care centers, professional offices of health care providers, and gymnasiums.[135] Religious institutions or entities controlled by religious institutions are not included on the list.

There are some limitations on the nondiscrimination requirements, and a failure to remove architectural barriers is not a violation unless such a removal is "readily achievable."[136] "Readily achievable" is defined as meaning "easily accomplishable and able to be carried out without much difficulty or expense."[137] Reasonable modifications in practices, policies or procedures are required unless they would fundamentally alter the nature of the goods, services, facilities, or privileges or they would result in an undue burden.[138] An undue burden is defined as an action involving "significant difficulty or expense."[139]

Title III contains a specific exemption for religious entities.[140] This applies when an entity is controlled by a religious entity. For example, a preschool that is run by a religious entity would not be covered under the ADA; however a preschool that is not run by a religious entity but that rents space from the religious entity, would be covered by Title III.

Similarly, Title III does not apply to private clubs or establishments exempted from coverage under Title II of the Civil Rights Act of 1964.[141] In interpreting this provision,[142] the Department of Justice has noted that courts have been most inclined to find private club status in cases where (1) members exercise a high degree of control over club operations, (2) the membership selection process is highly selective, (3) substantial membership fees are charged, (4) the entity is operated on a nonprofit basis, and (5) the club was not founded specifically to avoid compliance with federal civil rights law. Facilities of a private club lose their exemption, however, to the extent that they are made available for use by nonmembers as places of public accommodation.[143]

Title III also contains provisions relating to the prohibition of discrimination in public transportation services provided by private entities. Purchases of over-the-road buses are to be made in accordance with regulations issued by the Secretary of Transportation.[144]

The Department of Justice promulgated amendments to the Title III regulations that were amended as published in the *Federal Register* on September 15, 2010.[145] The amended Title III regulations adopt accessibility standards consistent with the new minimum guidelines and requirements issued by the Architectural and Transportation Barriers Compliance Board

(Access Board). In addition, the regulations include more detailed standards for service animals[146] and power-driven mobility devices, ticketing, and effective communication,[147] and provide for an element by element "safe harbor" in certain circumstances. The amended regulations took effect March 15, 2011, but compliance with the 2010 standards for accessible design is not required until March 15, 2012.

Bragdon v. Abbott and Direct Threats to Health and Safety

The nondiscrimination mandate of Title III does not require that an entity permit an individual to participate in or benefit from the services of a public accommodation where such an individual poses a direct threat to the health or safety of others.[148] This issue was discussed by the Supreme Court in *Bragdon v. Abbott, supra,* where the Court stated that "the existence, or nonexistence, of a significant risk must be determined from the standpoint of the person who refuses the treatment or accommodation, and the risk assessment must be based on medical or other objective evidence." Dr. Bragdon had the duty to assess the risk of infection "based on the objective, scientific information available to him and others in his profession. His belief that a significant risk existed, even if maintained in good faith, would not relieve him from liability." The Supreme Court remanded the case for further consideration of the direct threat issue. On remand, the First Circuit Court of Appeals held that summary judgment was warranted finding that Dr. Bragdon's evidence was too speculative or too tangential to create a genuine issue of fact.[149]

The Supreme Court declined to review a Fourth Circuit Court of Appeals decision regarding the direct threat exception to Title III. In *Montalvo v. Radcliffe,*[150] the Fourth Circuit held that excluding a child who has HIV from karate classes did not violate the ADA because the child posed a significant risk to the health and safety of others which could not be eliminated by reasonable modification.

Martin v. PGA Tour and "Fundamental Alteration"

In *Martin v. PGA Tour,* the Supreme Court in a 7-2 decision by Justice Stevens held that the ADA's requirements for equal access gave a golfer with a mobility impairment the right to use a golf cart in professional competitions.[151] The Ninth Circuit had ruled that the use of the cart was permissible since it did not "fundamentally alter" the nature of the competition.[152]

Title III of the ADA defines the term "public accommodation," specifically listing golf courses.[153] The majority opinion looked at this definition and the general intent of the ADA to find that golf tours and their qualifying rounds "fit comfortably within the coverage of Title III." The Court then discussed whether there was a violation of the substantive nondiscrimination provision of Title III. The ADA states that discrimination includes "a failure to make reasonable modifications in policies, practices, or procedures, when such modifications are necessary to afford such goods, services, facilities, privileges, advantages, or accommodations to individuals with disabilities, unless the entity can demonstrate that making such modifications would fundamentally alter the nature of such goods, services, facilities, privileges, advantages, or accommodations."[154]

In theory, the Court opined, there might be a fundamental alteration of a golf tournament in two ways: (1) an alteration in an essential aspect of the game, such as changing the diameter of the hole, might be unacceptable even if it affected all players equally, or (2) a less significant change that has only a peripheral impact on the game might give a golfer with a disability an advantage over others and therefore fundamentally alter the rules of competition. Looking at both these types of situations, Justice Stevens found that a waiver of the walking rule for Casey Martin did not amount to a fundamental alteration. He noted that the essence of the game was shot-making and that the walking rule was not an indispensable feature of tournament golf as golf carts are allowed on the Senior PGA Tour as well as certain qualifying events. In addition, Justice Stevens found that the fatigue from walking the approximately five miles over five hours was not significant. Regarding the question of whether allowing Casey Martin to use a cart would give him an advantage, the majority observed that an individualized inquiry must be made concerning whether a specific modification for a particular person's disability would be reasonable under the circumstances and yet not be a fundamental alteration. In examining the situation presented, the majority found that Casey Martin endured greater fatigue even with a cart than other contenders do by walking.

Justice Scalia, joined by Justice Thomas, wrote a scathing dissent describing the majority's opinion as distorting the text of Title III, the structure of the ADA, and common sense. The dissenters contended that Title III of the ADA applies only to particular places and persons and does not extend to golf tournaments. The dissent also contended that "the rules are the rules," that they are by nature arbitrary, and there is no basis for determining any of them "non-essential."

Spector v. Norwegian Cruise Line, Ltd. and the Application of the ADA to Foreign Cruise Ships

The Supreme Court in *Spector v. Norwegian Cruise Line, Ltd.* held in a decision written by Justice Kennedy that the ADA applies to companies that operate foreign cruise ships in U.S. waters.[155] Prior to this decision there had been a split in the circuits with the Eleventh Circuit holding in *Stevens v. Premier Cruises Inc.*[156] that Title III of the ADA does apply to foreign cruise ships and the Fifth Circuit in *Spector v. Norwegian Cruise Lines*[157] holding that the ADA would not be applicable since applicability would impose U.S. law on foreign nations. The Supreme Court's decision specifically held that the statute is applicable to foreign ships in the United States waters to the same extent that it is applicable to American ships in those waters. The majority concurred that cruise ships need not comply with the ADA if modifications would conflict with international legal obligations since the ADA only requires "readily achievable" accommodations. The 5-4 decision, however, was fragmented with various Justices joining for various aspects of the opinion. It is difficult, therefore, to determine exactly what type of accommodations would be required by the application of the ADA. Since the case below had been dismissed without a trial, it was remanded to determine the statutory requirements in this particular situation. The question of whether Title III requires any permanent and significant structural modifications that interfere with the international affairs of any cruise ship, foreign flag or domestic, was specifically left undecided. Justice Scalia, in his dissenting opinion, argued that the ADA should not be interpreted to apply in the absence of a clear statement from Congress.

ADA and the Internet

The ADA was enacted in 1990, prior to widespread use of the Internet, and does not specifically cover the Internet.[158] Similarly, the ADA regulations do not specifically mention the Internet. However, the Department of Justice has indicated that it believes the ADA does require Internet accessibility,[159] and has issued an advanced notice of rulemaking (ANPR) stating that it is considering revising the regulations implementing Titles II and III of the ADA to establish specific requirements for state and local governments and public accommodations to make their websites accessible to individuals with disabilities.[160] In a hearing in the 111th Congress, DOJ testified that although the ADA does not specifically mention the Internet, access to the Internet is a civil rights issue. DOJ further stated,

> the websites of entities covered by both Title II and Title III of the statute are required by law to ensure that their sites are fully accessible to individuals with disabilities. The Department is considering issuing guidance on the range of issues that arise with regard to the internet sites of private businesses that are public accommodations covered by Title III of the ADA. In so doing, the Department will solicit public comment from the broad range of parties interested in this issue.[161]

Although the ADA was amended in 2008 to respond to a series of Supreme Court decisions that had interpreted the definition of disability narrowly it did not address the issue of Internet coverage.[162] There has been no Supreme Court decision on point, and there have been few lower court judicial decisions. The lower courts that have examined the issue have split, creating some uncertainty. In addition, the use of a "nexus" approach in *National Federation of the Blind v. Target Corporation*,[163] requiring a connection between the Internet services and the physical place in order to present an actionable ADA claim, would limit the application of the ADA to on-line retailers. Despite this uncertainty, it would appear likely that the Department of Justice's position would prevail, especially in light of the ADA's broad nondiscrimination mandate.

The question of ADA coverage of internet sites will undoubtedly continue to be a closely watched issue.[164] It should be noted that this issue does not effect the requirement that federal government websites be accessible since the federal requirement is contained in a separate statute, Section 508 of the Rehabilitation Act.[165]

Vexatious Litigation

An issue which has prompted the introduction of bills in the last several Congresses involves the filing of multiple law suits by an individual with a disability based on de minimis violations and seeking money for a settlement.[166] Although these cases are seldom tried in court, *Molski v.*

Mandarin Touch Restaurant[167] did result in an opinion finding that the plaintiff was a vexatious litigant who filed hundreds of law suits designed to harass and intimidate business owners into agreeing to cash settlements. The district court ordered the plaintiff to obtain the leave of the court prior to filing any other claims under the ADA. In a related suit, the California district court also found against the counsel in the *Molski* case holding that the counsel was required to seek leave of the court before filing any additional ADA claims.[168]

These two cases were upheld on appeal to the Ninth Circuit in *Molski v. Evergreen Dynasty Corp.*[169] After a detailed examination of the cases in light of standards for vexatious litigation, the Ninth Circuit noted the following:

> For the ADA to yield its promise of equal access for the disabled, it may indeed be necessary and desirable for committed individuals to bring serial litigation advancing the time when public accommodations will be compliant with the ADA. But as important as this goal is to disabled individuals and to the public, serial litigation can become vexatious when, as here, a large number of nearly-identical complaints contain factual allegations that are contrived, exaggerated, and defy common sense.[170]

Similarly, the court of appeals held that the district court was within its discretion to impose a prefiling order. The Ninth Circuit observed "[t]hat the Frankovich Group filed numerous complaints containing false factual allegations, thereby enabled Molski's vexatious litigation, provided the district court with sufficient grounds on which to base its discretionary imposition of sanctions."[171]

Other Judicial Decisions

In *Ford v. Schering-Plough Corporation,*[172] the Third Circuit found a disparity in benefits for physical and mental illnesses did not violate the ADA and found that the disability benefits at issue did not fall within Title III. The court stated "This is in keeping with the host of examples of public accommodations provided by the ADA, all of which refer to places."[173] This conclusion was found to be in keeping with judicial decisions under Title II of the Civil Rights Act of 1964, 42 U.S.C. §2000(a).

Another issue under Title III is whether franchisers are subject to the Title. In *Nef v. American Dairy Queen Corp.,* the Fifth Circuit Court of Appeals found that a franchiser with limited control over the store a franchisee runs is not covered under Title III of the ADA.[174]

Remedies

The remedies and procedures of Title II of the Civil Rights Act of 1964 are incorporated in Title III of the ADA. Title II of the Civil Rights Act has generally been interpreted to include injunctive relief, not damages. In addition, state and local governments can apply to the Attorney General to certify that state or local building codes meet or exceed the minimum accessibility requirements of the ADA. The Attorney General may bring pattern or practice suits with a maximum civil penalty of $50,000 for the first violation and $100,000 for a violation in a subsequent case. The monetary damages sought by the Attorney General do not include punitive damages. Courts may also consider an entity's "good faith" efforts in considering the amount of the civil penalty. Factors to be considered in determining good faith include whether an entity could have reasonably anticipated the need for an appropriate type of auxiliary aid to accommodate the unique needs of a particular individual with a disability. Regulations relating to public accommodations have been promulgated by the Department of Justice[175] and regulations relating to the transportation provisions of Title III have been promulgated by the Department of Transportation.[176]

TELECOMMUNICATIONS

Title IV of the ADA amends Title II of the Communications Act of 1934[177] by adding a section providing that the Federal Communications Commission shall ensure that interstate and intrastate telecommunications relay services are available, to the extent possible and in the most efficient manner, to hearing impaired and speech impaired individuals. Any television public service announcement that is produced or funded in whole or part by any agency or instrumentality of the federal government shall include closed captioning of the verbal content of the announcement. The FCC is given enforcement authority with certain exceptions.[178]

TITLE V

Statutory Provisions

Title V contains an amalgam of provisions, several of which generated considerable controversy during ADA debate. In addition, the ADA Amendments Act of 2008 contained some additions to Title V.

Section 501 concerns the relationship of the ADA to other statutes and bodies of law. Subpart (a) states that "except as otherwise provided in this act, nothing in the act shall be construed to apply a lesser standard than the standards applied under Title V of the Rehabilitation Act ... or the regulations issued by Federal agencies pursuant to such Title." Subpart (b) provides that nothing in the act shall be construed to invalidate or limit the remedies, rights, and procedures of any federal, state, or local law that provides greater or equal protection. Nothing in the act is to be construed to preclude the prohibition of or restrictions on smoking. Subpart (d) provides that the act does not require an individual with a disability to accept an accommodation which that individual chooses not to accept.[179]

Subpart (c) of Section 501 limits the application of the act with respect to the coverage of insurance; however, the subsection may not be used as a subterfuge to evade the purposes of Titles I and III. The exact parameters of insurance coverage under the ADA are somewhat uncertain. As the EEOC has stated: "the interplay between the nondiscrimination principles of the ADA and employer provided health insurance, which is predicated on the ability to make health- related distinctions, is both unique and complex."[180] The Eighth Circuit Court of Appeals in *Henderson v. Bodine Aluminum, Inc.* issued a preliminary injunction compelling the plaintiff's employer to pay for chemotherapy that required an autologous bone marrow transplant.[181] The plaintiff was diagnosed with an aggressive form of breast cancer and her oncologist recommended entry into a clinical trial that randomly assigns half of its participants to high dose chemotherapy that necessitates an autologous bone marrow transplant. Because of the possibility that the plaintiff might have the more expensive bone marrow treatment, the employer's health plan refused to precertify the placement noting that the policy covered high dose chemotherapy only for certain types of cancer, not breast cancer. The court concluded that, "if the evidence shows that a given treatment is non-experimental—that is, if it is widespread, safe, and a significant improvement on traditional therapies—and the plan provides the treatment for other conditions directly comparable to the one at issue, the denial of treatment violates the ADA."[182]

The ADA Amendments Act made several additions to Section 501. The act states that the ADA does not alter eligibility standards for benefits under state workers' compensation laws or under state or federal disability benefit programs. P.L. 110-325 also states that nothing in the act alters the provision of Section 302(b)(2)(A)(ii),[183] specifying that reasonable modifications in policies, practices, or procedures shall be required, unless an entity can demonstrate that making such modifications in policies, practices, or procedures, including academic requirements in postsecondary education, would fundamentally alter the nature of the goods, services, facilities, privileges, advantages, or accommodations involved. The Senate Statement of Managers notes that this provision was added at the request of the higher education community and "is included solely to provide assurances that the bill does not alter current law with regard to the obligations of academic institutions under the ADA, which we believe is already demonstrated in case law on this topic."[184] The Managers' Statement also noted that this provision "is unrelated to the purpose of this legislation and should be given no meaning in interpreting the definition of disability."[185]

The ADA Amendments Act specifically prohibits reverse discrimination claims and states that nothing in the act shall provide the basis for a claim by a person without a disability that he or she was subject to discrimination because of a lack of a disability. The rules of construction provide that a covered entity under Title I, a public entity under Title II, or a person who operates a place of public accommodation under Title III, need not provide a reasonable accommodation or a reasonable modification to policies, practices, or procedures to an individual who meets the definition of disability solely under the "regarded as" prong of the definition.

Section 502 abrogates the Eleventh Amendment state immunity from suit and was discussed previously. Section 503 prohibits retaliation and coercion against an individual who has opposed an act or practice made unlawful by the ADA and was amended by the Lilly Ledbetter Fair Pay Act, P.L. 111-2, to allow for increased compensation in cases of discrimination. Section 504 requires the Architectural and Transportation Barriers Compliance Board (ATBCB) to issue guidelines regarding accessibility. Section 505 provides for attorneys' fees in "any action or administrative proceeding" under the act. Section 506, added by the ADA Amendments Act, states that "[t]he authority to issue regulations granted to the Equal Employment Opportunity

Commission, the Attorney General, and the Secretary of Transportation under this Act, includes the authority to issue regulations implementing the definitions contained in sections 3 and 4." Section 507 provides for technical assistance to help entities covered by the act in understanding their responsibilities. Section 508 provides for a study by the National Council on Disability regarding wilderness designations and wilderness land management practices and "reaffirms" that nothing in the Wilderness Act is to be construed as prohibiting the use of a wheelchair in a wilderness area by an individual whose disability requires the use of a wheelchair. Section 514 provides that "where appropriate and to the extent authorized by law, the use of alternative means of dispute resolution ... is encouraged...."[186] Section 515 provides for severability of any provision of the act that is found to be unconstitutional.

The coverage of Congress was a major controversy during the House-Senate conference on the ADA. Although the original language of the ADA did provide for some coverage of the legislative branch, Congress expanded upon this in the Congressional Accountability Act, P.L. 104-1. The major area of expansion was the incorporation of remedies that were analogous to those in the ADA applicable to the private sector.[187]

Buckhannon Board and Care Home, Inc. v. West Virginia and Attorneys' Fees

Section 505 of the ADA provides for attorneys' fees in "any action or administrative proceeding" under the act. This section was the subject of a Supreme Court decision in *Buckhannon Board and Care Home, Inc., v. West Virginia Department of Human Resources.*[188] In *Buckhannon,* the Supreme Court addressed the "catalyst theory" of attorneys' fees which posits that a plaintiff is a prevailing party if the lawsuit brings about a voluntary change in the defendant's conduct. The Court rejected this theory finding that attorneys' fees are only available where there is a judicially sanctioned change in the legal relationship of the parties.

Statutes providing for the award of attorneys' fees allow courts to make the awards to the "prevailing party." The question presented in *Buckhannon* was whether the term "prevailing party" includes a party who did not secure a judgment on the merits or a court-ordered consent decree, but has nonetheless achieved the desired result because the lawsuit has brought about a voluntary change in the defendant's conduct. The Court, in an opinion by then Chief

Justice Rehnquist, examined the ADA and the Fair Housing Amendments Act (FHAA)[189] and held that the term "prevailing party" cannot be interpreted in this manner, thus rejecting the concept of a "catalyst theory." Four other members of the Court, Justices O'Connor, Scalia, Kennedy, and Thomas joined with the Chief Justice while Justices Ginsburg, Stevens, Souter and Breyer dissented.

The Court first noted that in the United States parties are ordinarily required to bear their own attorneys' fees but that Congress has authorized the award of attorneys' fees in numerous statutes in addition to the ones at issue in *Buckhannon.* These fee-shifting provisions have been interpreted in the same manner and the Court noted, citing to *Hensley v. Eckerhart,*[190] that it approached the attorneys' fees provisions of the ADA and the FHAA in this manner.

Examining prior Supreme Court cases, Chief Justice Rehnquist found that a party receiving a judgment on the merits would clearly have a basis on which attorneys' fees might be awarded. Similarly, the court found that settlement agreements enforced through a consent decree may serve as the basis for an award of attorneys' fees. The catalyst theory was seen as dissimilar from these examples since "it allows an award where there is no judicially sanctioned change in the legal relationship of the parties."[191] A voluntary change, even if it accomplished what the plaintiff sought, the Court found, "lacks the necessary judicial *imprimatur* on the change."[192]

LEGISLATION RELATING TO THE ADA IN THE 112TH CONGRESS

Changes in the ADA's statutory language to address the issue of vexatious law suits have been proposed since the 106th Congress.[193] Proponents of such legislation have argued that notification requirements would help prevent the filing of suits designed to generate money for plaintiffs and law firms.[194] Those opposed to the legislation have argued that it would undermine enforcement of the ADA and that vexatious suits are best dealt with by state bar disciplinary procedures or by the courts.[195]

On March 2, 2011, Representative Hunter introduced H.R. 881, the ADA Notification Act of 2011. H.R. 881 would add provisions to the remedies and procedures of Title III of the ADA requiring a plaintiff to provide notice of an alleged violation to the defendant by registered mail. If such notice is not provided, the bill would eliminate state or federal court jurisdiction for the action.

End Notes

[1] The ADA and Section 504 of the Rehabilitation Act of 1973, however, have not been found to cover medical treatment decisions. See e.g. *Burger v. Bloomberg*, 418 F.3d 882 (8th Cir. 2005); *McElroy v. Patient Selection Committee of the Nebraska Medical Center*, 2007 U.S. Dist. LEXIS 86321 (D. Nebraska November 21, 2007)(an individual with mental illness was denied a kidney transplant on medical grounds).

[2] 42 U.S.C. §12102(b)(1).

[3] For a more detailed discussion of P.L. 110-325, see CRS Report RL34691, *The ADA Amendments Act: P.L. 110-325*, by Emily C. Barbour and James V. DeBergh.

[4] The ADA cases decided by the Supreme Court are: *Bragdon v. Abbott*, 524 U.S. 624 (1998); *Pennsylvania Department of Prisons v. Yeskey*, 524 U.S. 206 (1998); *Wright v. Universal Maritime Service Corp.*, 525 U.S. 70 (1998); *Cleveland v. Policy Management Systems*, 526 U.S. 795 (1999); *Olmstead v. L.C.*, 527 U.S. 581 (1999); *Murphy v. United Parcel Service, Inc.*, 527 U.S. 516 (1999); *Sutton v. United Air Lines, Inc.*, 527 U.S. 471(1999); *Albertson's Inc. v. Kirkingburg*, 527 U.S. 555 (1999); *Garrett v. University of Alabama*, 531 U.S. 356 (2001); *PGA Tour v. Martin*, 532 U.S. 661 (2001); *Buckhannon Board and Care Home, Inc. v. West Virginia Department of Human Resources*, 532 U.S. 598 (2001); *U.S. Airways Inc. v. Barnett*, 535 U.S. 391 (2002); *Toyota Motor Manufacturing v. Williams*, 534 U.S. 184 (2002); *Chevron USA Inc. v. Echazabal*, 536 U.S. 73 (2002); *Barnes v. Gorman*, 536 U.S. 181(2002); *Clackamas Gastroenterology Associates, P.C. v. Wells*, 538 U.S 440 (2003); *Tennessee v. Lane*, 541 U.S. 509 (2004); *Raytheon Co. v. Hernandez*, 540 U.S. 44 (2003); *Spector v. Norwegian Cruise Line, Ltd.*, 545 U.S. 119 (2005); and *United States v. Georgia*, 546 U.S. 151 (2006). For a discussion limited to Supreme Court decisions on the ADA, see CRS Report RL31401, *The Americans with Disabilities Act: Supreme Court Decisions*, by Nancy Lee Jones.

[5] 546 U.S. 151 (2006).

[6] *Arbaugh v. Y.& H. Corp.*, 546 U.S. 500 (2006).

[7] 486 F.3d 480 (8th Cir. 2007), *cert. granted*, 552 U.S. 1074 (2007); *cert. dismissed*, 552 U.S. 1136 (2008).

[8] See e.g., *Smith v. Midland Brake, Inc.*, 180 F.3d 1154 (10th Cir. 1999), holding that a vacant position automatically goes to a qualified individual with a disability; *EEOC v. Humiston-Keeling, Inc.*, 227 F.3d 1024 (7th Cir. 2000), holding that an employer does not have to "turn away a superior applicant."

[9] 29 U.S.C. §794. For a more detailed discussion of Section 504, see CRS Report RL34041, *Section 504 of the Rehabilitation Act of 1973: Prohibiting Discrimination Against Individuals with Disabilities in Programs or Activities Receiving Federal Assistance*, by Emily C. Barbour.

[10] 42 U.S.C. §12201(a).

[11] 42 U.S.C. §12206.

[12] See CRS Report RS21006, *Business Tax Provisions That Benefit Persons with Disabilities*, by Pamela J. Jackson, and CRS Report RS20555, *Additional Standard Tax Deduction for the Blind: A Description and Assessment*, by Pamela J. Jackson and Jennifer Teefy. See also GAO Report GAO-03-39, "Business Tax Incentives: Incentives to Employ Workers with Disabilities Receive Limited Use and Have an Uncertain Impact" (December 2002).

[13] The issue of whether the ADA definition of disability would cover individuals who are discriminated against due to a genetic condition is of less importance since the enactment of

the Genetic Information Nondiscrimination Act of 2008 (GINA), P.L. 110-233. For a discussion of this act, see CRS Report RL34584, *The Genetic Information Nondiscrimination Act of 2008 (GINA)*, by Amanda K. Sarata and James V. DeBergh, and CRS Report R40116, *The Genetic Information Nondiscrimination Act of 2008: Selected Issues*, by Amanda K. Sarata.

[14] 42 U.S.C. §12102(3) as amended by P.L. 110-325, §4(a). For a more detailed discussion of these amendments, see CRS Report RL34691, *The ADA Amendments Act: P.L. 110-325*, by Emily C. Barbour and James V. DeBergh.

[15] Low vision devices are not included in the ordinary eyeglasses and contact lens exception.

[16] New 29 C.F.R. §1630.2(j)(3)(iii); 76 *Federal Register* 17001 (March 25, 2011). For an analysis of the final regulations, CRS Report R41757, *The ADA Amendments Act Definition of Disability: Final EEOC Regulations* , by James V. DeBergh.

[17] 527 U.S. 471 (1999).

[18] 534 U.S. 184 (2004).

[19] 76 *Federal Register* 16978 (March 25, 2011). For an analysis of the final regulations, CRS Report R41757, *The ADA Amendments Act Definition of Disability: Final EEOC Regulations* , by James V. DeBergh.

[20] H.Rept. 110-730, Part 2, at 16 (2008).

[21] 270 F.3d 445 (7th Cir. 2001).

[22] Title I of the ADA covers employment, Title II covers states and localities, and Title III covers places of public accommodations such as grocery stores, doctors' offices, and movie theaters.

[23] 42 U.S.C. §12210.

[24] H.Rept. 101-596, 101st Cong., 2d Sess. 64; 1990 U.S. Code Cong. & Ad. News 573.

[25] *Id.*

[26] 42 U.S.C. §12208.

[27] 42 U.S.C. §12211.

[28] 524 U.S. 624 (1998). For a more detailed discussion of this decision, see CRS Report 98-599, *The Americans with Disabilities Act: HIV Infection is Covered Under the Act*, by Nancy Lee Jones.

[29] 527 U.S. 471 (1999). *Toyota Motor Manufacturing v. Williams*, 534 U.S. 184 (2004).

[30] 527 U.S. 516 (1999).

[31] 527 U.S. 555 (1999).

[32] 534 U.S. 184 (2002).

[33] 524 U.S. 624 (1998).

[34] Another major issue addressed in *Bragdon* involved the interpretation of the ADA's direct threat exemption which will be discussed in the section on public accommodations. For a more detailed discussion of *Bragdon*, see CRS Report 98-599, *The Americans with Disabilities Act: HIV Infection is Covered Under the Act*, by Nancy Lee Jones.

[35] 527 U.S. 666 (1999) (The Trademark Remedy Clarification Act, TRCA, which subjected states to suit for false and misleading advertising, did not validly abrogate state sovereign immunity; neither the right to be free from a business competitor's false advertising nor a more generalized right to be secure in one's business interests qualifies as a property right protected by the Due Process Clause).

[36] 527 U.S. 627 (1999)(Congress may abrogate state sovereign immunity but must do so through legislation that is appropriate within the meaning of Section 5 of the Fourteenth Amendment; Congress must identify conduct that violates the Fourteenth Amendment and must tailor its legislation to remedying or preventing such conduct).

[37] 528 U.S. 62 (2000).

[38] 42 U.S.C. §12101(b)(4). The Commerce Clause would not be sufficient authority on which to abrogate state sovereign immunity since the Supreme Court's decision in *Seminole Tribe of Florida v. Florida*, 517 U.S. 44 (1996).

[39] 42 U.S.C. §12202.

[40] It should be noted that the Eleventh Amendment applies only to states, not municipalities. See e.g., *Ability Center of Greater Toledo v. City of Sandusky*, 385 F.3d 901 (6th Cir. 2004).

[41] 546 U.S. 151 (2006).

[42] 42 U.S.C. §12112(a), as amended by P.L. 110-325, §5. The ADA Amendments Act strikes the prohibition of discrimination against a qualified individual with a disability because of the disability of such individual and substitutes the prohibition of discrimination against a qualified individual "on the basis of disability." The Senate Managers' Statement noted that this change "ensures that the emphasis in questions of disability discrimination is properly on the critical inquiry of whether a qualified person has been discriminated against on the basis of disability, and not unduly focused on the preliminary question of whether a particular person is a 'person with a disability.'" 153 CONG. REC. S.8347 (September 11, 2008)(Statement of Managers to Accompany S. 3406, the Americans with Disabilities Act Amendments Act of 2008). Two courts of appeal have held that the prohibition of discrimination in the "terms, conditions, or privileges of employment" creates a viable cause of action for disability-based harassment. See *Flowers v. Southern Reg'l Physician Servs, Inc.*, 247 F.3d 229 (5th Cir. 2001); *Fox v. General Motors Corp.*, 247 F.3d 169 (4th Cir. 2001); *Shaver v. Independent Stave Co.*, 350 F.3d 716 (8th Cir. 2003).

[43] 42 U.S.C. §12111(5).

[44] *Arbaugh v. Y. & H. Corp.*, 546 U.S. 500 (2006).

[45] 42 U.S.C. §2000e(b).

[46] P.L. 102-166 added this provision.

[47] 42 U.S.C. §1211(8). The EEOC has stated that a function may be essential because (1) the position exists to perform the duty, (2) there are a limited number of employees available who could perform the function, or (3) the function is highly specialized. 29 C.F.R. §1630(n)(2). A number of issues have been litigated concerning essential functions. For example, some courts have found that regular attendance is an essential function of most jobs. See e.g., *Carr v. Reno*, 23 F.3d 525 (D.C.Cir. 1994), *Brenneman v. Medcentral Health System*, 366 F.3d 412 (6th Cir. 2004), *cert. denied*, 543 U.S. 1114 (2005)("the record is replete with evidence of plaintiff's excessive absenteeism, which rendered him unqualified for that position.") In *Mulloy v. Acushnet Co.*, 460 F.3d 141 (1st Cir. 2006), the first circuit found that an essential function of the job at issue included being physically present at the plant in order to perform troubleshooting and take corrective actions and found that the plaintiff could not perform the job's essential functions remotely. In *Frazier v. Simmons*, 254 F.3d 1247 (10th Cir. 2001), the tenth circuit held that a crime investigator with MS was not otherwise qualified to perform his job duties since it would be very difficult for him to stand or walk for prolonged periods, to run or to physically restrain persons. Similarly, a nurse with a back injury that prevented her from lifting more than 15 or 20 pounds was not a qualified individual with a disability since the ability to lift fifty pounds was an essential function of her job. *Phelps v. Optima Health, Inc.*, 251 F.3d 21 (1st Cir. 2001).

[48] See 45 C.F.R. Part 84.

[49] 42 U.S.C. §12111(9).

[50] 42 U.S.C. §12111(10).

[51] EEOC, "EEOC Enforcement Guidance on Reasonable Accommodation and Undue Hardship Under the Americans with Disabilities Act," No. 915.002 (March 1, 1999).

[52] http://www.eeoc.gov/policy/docs/accommodation.html#requesting.

[53] It should be emphasized that the EEOC's guidance does **not** have the force of regulations and courts are not bound to follow the guidance although some courts do defer to agency expertise.

[54] 29 C.F.R. §1630.9.

[55] http://www.eeoc.gov/policy/docs/accommodation.html.

[56] 44 F.3d 538 (7th Cir. 1995).

[57] *Id.* At 542-543. See also *Schmidt v. Methodist Hospital of Indiana*, 89 F.3d 342 (7th Cir. 1996), where the court found that reasonable accommodation does not require an employer to provide everything an employee requests.
[58] 538 U.S. 440 (2003).
[59] 42 U.S.C. §12111(4).
[60] EEOC Compliance Manual §605:0009.
[61] 426 F.3d 887 (7th Cir. 2005).
[62] *Id.* at 892.
[63] 527 U.S. 555 (1999).
[64] 536 U.S. 73 (2002).
[65] 42 U.S.C. §12113(a).
[66] 42 U.S.C. §12113(b).
[67] 226 F.3d 1063 (9th Cir. 2000).
[68] 29 C.F.R. §1630.15(b)(2).
[69] 499 U.S. 187 (1991).
[70] For more information, see CRS Report RL30008, *Labor and Mandatory Arbitration Agreements: Background and Discussion*, by Jon O. Shimabukuro.
[71] 535 U.S. 391 (2002).
[72] 540 U.S. 44 (2003).
[73] Upon review, the Ninth Circuit Court of Appeals reversed and remanded the district court's grant of the employer's motion for summary judgment. *Hernandez v. Hughes Missile Systems Co.*, 362 F.3d 564 (9th Cir. 2004).
[74] 42 U.S.C. §12112.
[75] EEOC, "ADA Enforcement Guidance: Preemployment Disability-Related Questions and Medical Examinations," October 10, 1995.
[76] *Id.*
[77] 411 F.3d 831 (7th Cir. 2005). For a more detailed discussion of this case, see Maureen E. Mulvihill, "*Karraker v. Rent-a-Center:* Testing the Limits of the ADA, Personality Tests, and Employer Preemployment Screening," 37 LOY. U. CHI. L. J. 865 (2006).
[78] http://www.eeoc.gov/facts/evacuation.html. For a detailed discussion of emergency procedures for employees with disabilities, see Federal Emergency Management Agency, "Emergency Procedures for Employees with Disabilities in Office Occupancies." http://www.securitymanagement.com/library/disable.html.
[79] See http://www.eeoc.gov/facts/pandemic_flu.html. For a discussion of these issues, see CRS Report R40866, *The Americans with Disabilities Act (ADA): Employment Issues and the 2009 Influenza Pandemic*, by Nancy Lee Jones.
[80] 42 U.S.C. §12113(a).
[81] 42 U.S.C. §12113(c).
[82] 42 U.S.C. §12113(b).
[83] 29 C.F.R. §1630.2(r).
[84] 42 U.S.C. §12113(d)(1). This exception for religious organizations mirrors the exception provided in Title VII of the Civil Rights Act of 1964, which prohibits employment discrimination based on race, color, religion, national origin, or sex. *See* 42 U.S.C. §2000e et seq. For a legal analysis of the applicability of the exception, see CRS Report RS22745, *Religion and the Workplace: Legal Analysis of Title VII of the Civil Rights Act of 1964 as It Applies to Religion and Religious Organizations*, by Cynthia Brougher.
[85] 42 U.S.C. §12113(d)(2).
[86] Hosanna-Tabor Evangelical Lutheran Church and School v. EEOC, 132 S.Ct. 694 (2012).
[87] *Id.* at 710.
[88] *Id.* at 703 ("The Establishment Clause prevents the Government from appointing ministers, and the Free Exercise Clause prevents it from interfering with the freedom of religious groups to select their own [ministers].").
[89] 42 U.S.C. §12113(e)(2).

[90] *Id.* The Secretary of Health and Human Services maintains a list of infectious and communicable diseases transmitted through the food supply. *See* 74 *Federal Register* 61151 (November 23, 2009).

[91] 29 C.F.R. Appendix §1630.3.

[92] See e.g., *Shafer v. Preston Memorial Hospital Corp.*, 107 F.3d 274 (4th Cir. 1997)(individual is a current user if he or she has illegally used drugs "in a periodic fashion during the weeks and months prior to discharge.")

[93] 29 C.F.R. Appendix §1630.3.

[94] 42 U.S.C. §12114(c); 29 C.F.R. §1630.16(b)(4).

[95] EEOC Compliance Manual §902.2(c)(4). See also *Hamilton v. Southwestern Bell Telephone Co.*, 136 F.3d 1047 (5th Cir. 1998)("the ADA does not insulate emotional or violent outbursts blamed on an impairment").

[96] EEOC Enforcement Guidance on the ADA and Psychiatric Disabilities, No. 915.002, p. 29 (March 25, 1997).

[97] 42 U.S.C. §§2000e-4, 2000e-5, 2000e-6, 2000e-8, 2000e-9.

[98] In *Gagliardo v. Connaught Laboratories*, 311 F.3d 565 (3d Cir. 2002), an employee who claimed that she was discriminated against due to her multiple sclerosis won an award of $2.3 million despite the ADA caps. The court found that the judge had properly proportioned the claims between the federal and state causes of action and found that the fact that the state law did not contain a cap indicated that it was intended to provide a remedy beyond the federal remedies.

[99] 550 U.S. 618 (2007).

[100] For a discussion of the *Ledbetter* decision, see CRS Report RS22686, *Pay Discrimination Claims Under Title VII of the Civil Rights Act: A Legal Analysis of the Supreme Court's Decision in Ledbetter v. Goodyear Tire & Rubber Co., Inc.*, by Jody Feder. For a discussion of the legislation, see CRS Report RL31867, *Pay Equity Legislation*, by Benjamin Collins and Jody Feder.

[101] 527 U.S. 526 (1999).

[102] But see *Barnes v. Gorman*, 536 U.S. 181 (2002), where the Supreme Court held that punitive damages may not be awarded under Section 202 of the ADA.

[103] 187 F.3d 1241 (10th Cir. 1999).

[104] 42 U.S.C. §§12131-12133.

[105] 29 U.S.C. §794.

[106] 28 C.F.R. §35.150.

[107] *Id.* The Department of Justice provided a document containing examples of common ADA compliance problems by city governments that have been identified through the Department of Justice's ongoing enforcement efforts. See http://www.usdoj.gov/crt/ada/comprob.htm.

[108] 75 *Federal Register* 56207 (September 15, 2010). The Department of Justice amended existing Title II and Title III regulations. For a more detailed discussion of the safe harbor provision see CRS Report R41376, *The Americans with Disabilities Act (ADA): Final Rule Amending Title II and Title III Regulations*, by Emily C. Barbour and James V. DeBergh.

[109] For a more detailed discussion of the provisions relating to service animals see CRS Report R41468, *The Americans with Disabilities Act (ADA) and Service Animals*, by Emily C. Barbour.

[110] 75 *Federal Register* 56164 (September 15, 2010). For a more detailed discussion of the changes generally see CRS Report R41376, *The Americans with Disabilities Act (ADA): Final Rule Amending Title II and Title III Regulations*, by Emily C. Barbour and James V. DeBergh.

[111] http://www.usdoj.gov/crt/ada/emergencyprep.htm. For a more detailed discussion of these issues, see CRS Report RS22254, *The Americans with Disabilities Act and Emergency Preparedness and Response*, by Emily C. Barbour.

[112] 541 U.S. 509 (2004).

[113] 546 U.S. 151 (2006).

[114] The Supreme Court had remanded this case for consideration of whether Yeskey was an individual with a disability. On remand, the district court held that he was not covered by the ADA since he was not substantially limited in a major life activity. *Yeskey v. Pennsylvania Department of Corrections*, 76 F.Supp. 2d 572 (M.D. Pa.1999).

[115] *Olmstead* has focused federal and state attention on the development of policies that would expand home and community-based care for individuals with disabilities. For a more detailed discussion of *Olmstead*, see CRS Report R40106, *Olmstead v. L.C.: Judicial and Legislative Developments in the Law of Deinstitutionalization*, by Emily C. Barbour.

[116] See also *Frederick L., Nina S., Kevin C. And Steven F. v. Department of Public Welfare*, 422 F.3d 151 (3d Cir. 2005), where the court found that Pennsylvania's Department of Public Welfare was obligated to integrate eligible patients into local community-based settings and was required to articulate a commitment to this requirement in a specific comprehensive, effectively working, plan before it could utilize a "fundamental alteration" defense.

[117] *Crowder v. Kitagawa*, 81 F.3d 1480 (9th Cir. 1996). The court stated: "Although Hawaii's quarantine requirement applies equally to all persons entering the state with a dog, its enforcement burdens visually-impaired persons in a manner different and greater than it burdens others. Because of the unique dependence upon guide dogs among many of the visually-impaired, Hawaii's quarantine effectively denies these persons ... meaningful access to state services, programs, and activities while such services, programs, and activities remain open and easily accessible by others."

[118] In *Kinney v. Yerusalim*, 812 F.Supp. 547 (E.D. Pa. 1993), *aff'd* 9 F.3d 1067 (3d Cir. 1993), *cert. denied*, 511 U.S. 1033 (1994), the court found that street repair projects must include curb ramps for individuals with disabilities. Similarly, see *Ability Center of Greater Toledo v. Lechner*, 385 F.3d 901 (6th Cir. 2004), where the court held that Title II "does not merely prohibit intentional discrimination. It also imposes on public entities the requirement that they provide qualified disabled individuals with meaningful access to public services, which in certain instances necessitates that public entities take affirmative steps to remove architectural barriers to such access in the process of altering existing facilities." At 912. See also *Barden v. Sacramento*, 292 F.3d 1073 (9th Cir. 2002), *cert. denied*, 539 U.S. 958 (2003). See also 28 C.F.R. §35.151(e)(1), where the Department of Justice details the requirements for curb ramps.

[119] *Heather K. v. City of Mallard, Iowa*, 946 F.Supp. 1373 (N.D.Iowa 1996).

[120] *Innovative Health Systems, Inc. v. City of White Plains*, 117 F.3d 37 (2d Cir. 1997).

[121] 42 U.S.C. §§12141-12165. P.L. 104-287 added a new definition. The term "commuter rail transportation" has the meaning given the term "commuter rail passenger transportation" in 45 U.S.C. §502(9). For a more detailed discussion of the transportation provisions, see CRS Report RS22676, *Public Transportation Providers' Obligations Under the Americans with Disabilities Act (ADA)*, by Emily C. Barbour. Airplanes are covered by the Air Carriers Access Act, 49 U.S.C. §41705. For a discussion of this law, see CRS Report RL34047, *Overview of the Air Carrier Access Act (ACAA)*, by Emily C. Barbour.

[122] 42 U.S.C. §12143.

[123] 42 U.S.C. §12162.

[124] 70 *Federal Register* 70734 (November 23, 2005).

[125] 42 U.S.C. §12133.

[126] 28 C.F.R. Part 35.

[127] 49 C.F.R. Parts 27, 37, 38.

[128] 536 U.S. 181 (2002).

[129] 42 U.S.C. §12132. Section 203, 42 U.S.C. §12133, contains the enforcement provisions.

[130] 29 U.S.C. §794. Section 504 in relevant part prohibits discrimination against individuals with disabilities in any program or activity that receives federal financial assistance. The requirements of Section 504, its regulations, and judicial decisions were the model for the statutory language in the ADA where the nondiscrimination provisions are not limited to entities that receive federal financial assistance.

[131] 42 U.S.C. §2000d *et seq.*
[132] U.S. Const., Art. I §8, cl.1.
[133] *Pennhurst State School and Hospital v. Halderman*, 451 U.S. 1, 17 (1981).
[134] 42 U.S.C. §12182.
[135] 42 U.S.C. §12181.
[136] 42 U.S.C. §12182(b)(2)(A)(iv).
[137] 42 U.S.C. §12181.
[138] 42 U.S.C. §12182(b)(2)(A).
[139] 28 C.F.R. §36.104.
[140] 42 U.S.C. §12187.
[141] 42 U.S.C. §2000a-3(a).
[142] 42 U.S.C. 12187.
[143] Department of Justice, "ADA Title III Technical Assistance Manual" III-1.6000.
[144] 42 U.S.C. §12184. This section was amended by P.L. 104-59 to provide that accessibility requirements for private over-the-road buses must be met by small providers within three years after the issuance of final regulations and with respect to other providers, within two years after the issuance of such regulations.
[145] 75 *Federal Register* 56164 (September 15, 2010). For a more detailed discussion of the changes generally see CRS Report R41376, *The Americans with Disabilities Act (ADA): Final Rule Amending Title II and Title III Regulations*, by Emily C. Barbour and James V. DeBergh.
[146] For a more detailed discussion of the provisions relating to service animals see CRS Report R41468, *The Americans with Disabilities Act (ADA) and Service Animals*, by Emily C. Barbour.
[147] For a more detailed discussion the amended regulations regarding effective communication in the hospital setting see CRS Report 97-826, *Americans with Disabilities Act (ADA) Requirements Concerning the Provision of Interpreters by Hospitals and Doctors*, by James V. DeBergh. For a discussion of an advanced notice of proposed rulemaking (ANPR) regarding captioning see CRS Report R41659, *The Americans with Disabilities Act (ADA): Movie Captioning and Video Description*, by James V. DeBergh.
[148] For a more detailed discussion of this issue, see CRS Report RS22219, *The Americans with Disabilities Act (ADA) Coverage of Contagious Diseases*, by James V. DeBergh. The EEOC has discussed the concept of direct threat in the context of an influenza pandemic and determined that "[w]hether pandemic influenza rises to the level of a direct threat depends on the severity of the illness." http://www.eeoc.gov/facts/pandemic_flu.html.
[149] *Abbott v. Bragdon*, 163 F.3d 87 (1st Cir. 1998), *cert. denied*, 526 U.S. 1131 (1999).
[150] 167 F.3d 873 (4th Cir. 1999), *cert. denied*, 528 U.S. 813 (1999).
[151] 532 U.S. 661 (2001).
[152] 204 F.3d 994 (9th Cir. 2000).
[153] 42 U.S.C. §12181(7).
[154] 42 U.S.C. §12182(b)(2)(A)(ii)(emphasis added). The Department of Justice regulations echo the statutory language and provide the following illustration. "A health care provider may refer an individual with a disability to another provider if that individual is seeking, or requires, treatment or services outside of the referring provider's area of specialization, and if the referring provider would make a similar referral for an individual without a disability who seeks or requires the same treatment or services." 28 C.F.R. §36.302. The concept of fundamental alteration did not originate in the statutory language of the ADA but was derived from Supreme Court interpretation of Section 504 of the Rehabilitation Act of 1973, 29 U.S.C. §794, which, in part, prohibits discrimination against an individual with a disability in any program or activity that receives federal financial assistance and was the model on which the ADA was based. In *Southeastern Community College v. Davis*, 442 U.S. 397 (1979), the Supreme Court addressed a suit by a hearing impaired woman who wished to attend a college nursing program. The college rejected her application because it

believed her hearing disability made it impossible for her to participate safely in the normal clinical training program and to provide safe patient care. The Supreme Court found no violation of Section 504 and held that it did "not encompass the kind of curricular changes that would be necessary to accommodate respondent in the nursing program." Since Davis could not function in clinical courses without close supervision, the Court noted that the college would have had to limit her to academic courses. The Court further observed that "whatever benefits respondent might realize from such a course of study, she would not receive even a rough equivalent of the training a nursing program normally gives. Such a fundamental alteration in the nature of a program is far more than the 'modification' the regulation requires." (At 409-410.) In conclusion, the Court found that "nothing in the language or history of § 504 reflects an intention to limit the freedom of an educational institution to require reasonable physical qualifications for admission to a clinical training program." (At 414.)

155 545 U.S. 119 (2005).

156 215 F.3d 1237 (11th Cir. 2000), rehearing and rehearing en banc denied, 284 F.3d 1187 (11th Cir. 2002).

157 356 F.3d 641 (5th Cir. 2004).

158 For a more detailed discussion of this issue, see CRS Report R40462, *The Americans with Disabilities Act (ADA): Application to the Internet*, by James V. DeBergh. A similar issue is raised by electronic book readers. See http://www.ada.gov/kindle_ltr_eddoj.htm.

159 *Achieving the Promise of the Americans with Disabilities Act in the Digital Age: Current Issues, Challenges, and Opportunities: Hearing Before the H. Subcommittee on the Constitution, Civil Rights and Civil Liberties of the H. Comm. on the Judiciary*, 111th Cong., 2d Sess. (Testimony of Samuel R. Bagenstos, Principal Deputy Assistant Attorney General for Civil Rights, Department of Justice), http://judiciary.house.gov/hearings/pdf/Bagenstos100422.pdf.

160 http://www.ada.gov/anprm2010/web

161 *Id.*

162 The ADA Amendments Act, P.L. 110-325. For a more detailed discussion of P.L. 110-325, see CRS Report RL34691, *The ADA Amendments Act: P.L. 110-325*, by Emily C. Barbour and James V. DeBergh.

163 452 F.Supp.2d 946 (N.D. Calif. 2006). The case was settled on August 27, 2008. See http://www.nfb.org. For a more detailed discussion of this case, see Isabel Arana DuPree, "Websites as 'Places of Public Accommodation': Amending the Americans with Disabilities Act in the Wake of *National Federal of the Blind v. Target Corporation*," NC J. L. & Tech. 273 (2007); Jeffrey Bashaw, "Applying the Americans with Disabilities Act to Private Websites after *National Federation of the Blind v. Target*," 4 Shidler J. L. Com. & Tech. 3 (2008).

164 For a more detailed discussion of the issue, see National Council on Disability, "When the Americans with Disabilities Act Goes Online: Application of the ADA to the Internet and the Worldwide Web," (July 10, 2003) http://www.ncd.gov/newsroom/publications/2003/adainternet.htm; The Association of the Bar of the City of New York, "Website Accessibility for People with Disabilities," 62 The Record 118 (2007); Steven Mendelsohn, and Martin Gould, "When the Americans with Disabilities Act Goes Online: Application of the ADA to the Internet and the World Wide Web," 7 Comp. L. Rev. & Tech. J. 173 (2004).

165 29 U.S.C. §794(d), as amended by P.L. 105-220. Section 508 requires that the electronic and information technology used by federal agencies be accessible to individuals with disabilities, including employees and member of the public. Generally, Section 508 requires each federal department or agency and the U.S. Postal Service to ensure that individuals with disabilities who are federal employees have access to and use of electronic and information technology that is comparable to that of individuals who do not have disabilities. For more detailed information, see http://www.section508.gov.

[166] See section on legislation *infra.* See also CRS Report RS22296, *The Americans with Disabilities Act: Legislation Concerning Notification Prior to Initiating Legal Action*, by Emily C. Barbour. For a discussion of vexatious lawsuits, see Wayne C. Arnold and Lisa D. Herzog, "How Many Lawsuits Does It Take to Declare an ADA Plaintiff Vexatious?" 48 Orange County Lawyer 50 (July 2006).

[167] 347 F.Supp.2d 860 (C.D.Calif. 2004).

[168] *Molski v. Mandarin Touch Restaurant*, 359 F.Supp.2d 924 (C.D.Calif. 2005).

[169] 500 F.3d 1047 (9th Cir. 2007), cert. denied, 129 S. Ct. 594, 172 L. Ed. 2d 455 (2008).

[170] *Id.* at 38.

[171] *Id.* at 43.

[172] 145 F.3d 601(3d Cir. 1998), *cert. denied*, 525 U.S. 1093 (1999).

[173] *Id.* at 612.

[174] 58 F.3d 1063 (5th Cir. 1995), *cert. denied*, 516 U.S. 1045 (1996).

[175] 28 C.F.R. Part 36.

[176] 49 C.F.R. Parts 27, 37, 38.

[177] 47 U.S.C. §§201 *et seq.*

[178] 47 U.S.C. §255. For an FCC discussion of closed captioning, see http://www.fcc.gov/cgb/consumerfacts/closedcaption.html.

[179] 29 U.S.C. §§790 *et seq.*

[180] EEOC, "Interim Policy Guidance on ADA and Health Insurance," BNA's Americans with Disabilities Act Manual 70:1051 (June 8, 1993). This guidance deals solely with the ADA implications of disability-based health insurance plan distinctions and states that "insurance distinctions that are not based on disability, and that are applied equally to all insured employees, do not discriminate on the basis of disability and so do not violate the ADA."

[181] 70 F.3d 958 (8th Cir. 1995).

[182] See also *Rogers v. Department of Health and Environmental Control*, 174 F.3d 431 (4th Cir. 1999), where the fourth circuit court of appeals held that the ADA does not require employers to offer the same long-term disability insurance benefits for mental and physical disabilities. For a more detailed discussion of the ADA and coverage of mental and physical disabilities in insurance, see Matthew G. Simon, "Not All Illnesses Are Treated Equally - Does a Disability Benefits Plan Violate the ADA by Providing Less Generous Long-Term Benefits for Mentally Disabled Employees than for Physically Disabled Employees?" 8 U. Pa. J. Lab. & Emp. L. 943 (Summer 2006).

[183] 42 U.S.C. §12182(b)(2)(A)(ii).

[184] 153 CONG. REC. S. 8347 (September 11, 2008)(Statement of Managers to Accompany S. 3406) the Americans with Disabilities Act Amendments Act of 2008).

[185] *Id.*

[186] 42 U.S.C. §12212.

[187] Congress has also applied the employment and public accommodation provisions of the ADA to the Executive Office of the President. P.L. 104-331 (October 26, 1996).

[188] 532 U.S. 598 (2001).

[189] 42 U.S.C. §3613(c)(2).

[190] 461 U.S. 424 (1983).

[191] 532 U.S. 598, 605 (2001).

[192] *Id.*

[193] For a more detailed discussion, see CRS Report RS22296, *The Americans with Disabilities Act: Legislation Concerning Notification Prior to Initiating Legal Action*, by Emily C. Barbour; Carri Becker, "Private Enforcement of the Americans with Disabilities Act via Serial Litigation: Abusive or Commendable?," 17 Hastings Women's L.J. 93 (2006). See also the preceding discussion of judicial decisions under Title III, which have attempted to respond to the issue of vexatious litigants.

[194]See Testimony of the Honorable Mark Foley, hearing on H.R. 3590, The ADA Notification Act, Before the House Committee on the Judiciary, Subcommittee on the Constitution, May 18, 2000, published at http://www.house.gov/ judiciary/fole0518.htm.

[195]See Letter to Honorable Charles Canady, chairman, Subcommittee on the Constitution, House Committee on the Judiciary from Robert Raben, Assistant Attorney General, reprinted at http://commdocs.house.gov/committees/ judiciary/hju66728.000/hju66728_0f.htm.

In: The United Nations Convention …
Editor: Timo Wallner
ISBN: 978-1-62808-120-6

Chapter 10

SENATE CONSIDERATION OF TREATIES*

Valerie Heitshusen

The consideration of treaties and nominations constitutes the executive business of the Senate.[1] To conduct executive business, the Senate must resolve into executive session. Senate Rule XXIX governs executive sessions, generally; Rule XXX addresses proceedings on treaties.

When the President submits a treaty to the Senate, the treaty, and any supporting materials, are referred to the Committee on Foreign Relations. Paragraph 3 of Senate Rule XXIX requires that all treaties and "all remarks, votes, and proceedings thereon shall also be kept secret, until the Senate shall, by their resolution, take off the injunction of secrecy." At the time the treaty is referred to committee, the Senate typically agrees by unanimous consent to remove the "injunction of secrecy."[2]

The Foreign Relations Committee can order the treaty reported back to the Senate—favorably, unfavorably, or without recommendation—or, instead, decline to act on the treaty. If the committee does not act on the treaty, it is not automatically returned to the President. Treaties, unlike bills and other legislative measures, remain available to the Senate from one Congress to the next, until they are disposed or the Senate agrees to return them to the President. Paragraph 2 of Rule XXX states in part that "all proceedings on treaties shall terminate with the Congress, and they shall be resumed at the

* This is an edited, reformatted and augmented version of a Congressional Research Service publication, CRS Report for Congress 98-384, prepared for Members and Committees of Congress, from www.crs.gov, dated October 26, 2012.

commencement of the next Congress as if no proceedings had previously been had thereon." Thus, if the Foreign Relations Committee fails to report a treaty before the end of a Congress, the treaty remains before the committee during the next Congress. If the committee has reported a treaty, but the Senate has not completed floor consideration of it when the Congress ends, the treaty is recommitted to the committee, and the committee must report it again before the Senate may consider it on the floor.

If the committee votes to report a treaty, it is placed on the Senate's *Executive Calendar* and must lie over on this calendar for one day before possible floor consideration. The Senate may waive this layover requirement by unanimous consent.

When the Senate is prepared to consider the treaty, the majority leader makes either a unanimous consent request to that effect, or, while in legislative session, a non-debatable motion that the Senate go into executive session for the purpose of considering a specific treaty. If the Senate already is in executive session, or if the Senate agrees simply to resolve into executive session without a purpose for doing so being specified in the motion, then a motion made in executive session to proceed to any but the first item listed on the Executive Calendar is debatable, meaning that the motion to proceed could be subject to extended debate and perhaps the cloture procedures under Rule XXII.

Once the Senate has agreed to proceed to the treaty and is in executive session, the Senate first considers the text of the treaty itself, just as it would consider the text of a bill in legislative session. The treaty is amendable and it is open for amendment at any point, with any amendments proposed by the Foreign Relations Committee being considered first. Once the amending process (if any) is complete and there is no further debate or amendment, the Senate does not vote on approving the treaty. Instead, the Senate takes up a *resolution of ratification*, by which the Senate formally gives its advice and consent, empowering the President to proceed with the ratification of the treaty. This un-numbered resolution typically states: "*Resolved* (two-thirds of the Senators present concurring therein), That the Senate advise and consent to the ratification" of the treaty in question. When the resolution of ratification is presented to the Senate, it incorporates any amendments to the treaty that the Senate had previously approved.

One day is required to elapse between the time that the Senate completes action on the treaty itself and the time it begins consideration of the resolution of ratification, although this requirement also is frequently waived by unanimous consent. After the Senate has begun considering this resolution, amendments proposing to change the text of the treaty itself no longer are in order. Senators may amend the resolution of ratification, however, by attaching to it reservations, declarations, statements, or understandings that can affect the interpretation or implementation of the treaty. Again, the Senate first considers any reservation or other proposition that the Foreign Relations Committee has reported.

Under Article II, Section 2 of the Constitution, the final vote on agreeing to the resolution of ratification – with whatever reservations or other propositions may have been attached to it – a requires a vote of two-thirds of the Senators present and voting (a quorum being present). A two-thirds vote also is required to agree to a motion to postpone indefinitely further consideration of the treaty and accompanying resolution, because adopting that motion has the effect of disposing of the treaty permanently.

All other motions prior to final action, including those proposing treaty amendments or reservations, require only simple majority votes. Treaties, resolutions of ratification, reservations, and other related propositions are debatable under the normal rules of the Senate, and they are subject to the Senate's cloture rule, Rule XXII. When cloture is invoked on a resolution of ratification, action on all amendments and reservations must be completed before a vote on ratification under the rule's post-cloture 30-hour time limit.[3]

Frequently, the Senate agrees by unanimous consent to dispense with consideration of the treaty itself and proceeds immediately to consider the resolution of ratification.

For additional information, see *Riddick's Senate Procedure*, pp. 832-842 and 1294-1310; see also *Treaties and Other International Agreements: The Role of the United States Senate*, a committee print of the Senate Committee on Foreign Relations (S.Prt. 106-71), available at http://www.congress.gov/ senate/lists.html.

End Notes

[1] Article II, §2, clause 2, of the U.S. Constitution provides the Senate this advice and consent function.

[2] See, for example, Sen. Harry Reid, "Removal of Injunction of Secrecy - Treaty Document No. 112-5, Treaty Document No. 112-7, and Treaty Document 112-8," remarks in the Senate, Congressional Record, daily edition, May 17, 2012, p. S3292.

[3] For more information on the cloture process, generally, and the effects of invoking cloture, see CRS Report 98-425, Invoking Cloture in the Senate, by Christopher M. Davis, and CRS Report 98-780, Cloture: Its Effect on Senate Proceedings, by Walter J. Oleszek.

INDEX

B

C

D

E

F

G

H

I

N

O

P

T

U

V

W

Y